One on One With the Master

Virginia "Kitty" Ford

authorHOUSE®

AuthorHouse™
1663 Liberty Drive
Bloomington, IN 47403
www.authorhouse.com
Phone: 1-800-839-8640

First published by AuthorHouse 10/18/2010

ISBN: 978-1-4520-8495-4 (sc)
ISBN: 978-1-4520-8496-1 (e)

Library of Congress Control Number: 2010915068

Printed in the United States of America

This book is printed on acid-free paper.

Certain stock imagery © Thinkstock.

Dedication

Dedicated to my "Nanny" Aunt Marjorie Trice, who always believed in me.
Always encouraging me to be me, yet being the best at whatever I did.

To my "Auntie B" Aunt Alberta Trice, who taught me that life, is not always fun
and games and in the process of growing up, there comes responsibilities.

I love you both!

A Special Thank you
To Mrs. Lucretia Trice

Mrs. Trice took me under her wings and treats me like one of
her children. She is indeed a true woman of God.
God blessed me with the opportunity and the pleasure of knowing this
warm hearted, God fearing lady, a lady of wisdom and faithfulness.
Mother is who she is to me. The day you welcomed me into your home until this
day, you have always shown me love, you have taught me how to be a lady at all
times. Watching and listening to you singing praises unto God is such a joy to me.
Ma Trice is such a beautiful person inside and out, a meek and humble person. I
just want to say thank you because you treated me like I was part of your family.
I say thank you because you choose to love me in spite of my past and in spite of
what others said about me, I say thank you for your encouragement. I say thank
you for your prayers. I say thank you for your chastisement I say thank you for
sharing your wisdom. A very special thank you for sharing your love... I thank
God for placing you in my life. I just want you to know I love you much.

Acknowledgment

I want to thank God Almighty who allowed me to go through trials and tribulations in order that I could make it to what he had in store for me, *His plan and His purpose.*

I would like to take the time to thank Mr. Steve Harvey, whom I have never met. Mr. Harvey has inspired me to fulfill my dreams. Every morning on his radio show his first twelve minutes is giving God homage. Every morning he says Steve Harvey has a radio show. When he says this he is not boasting but what he is saying if he can do it so can you if we just get out of God's way and let him do what he do. This is for the thank you, Mr. Harvey also says God has no respective person just put your name where his name is and whatever you want God to bless you with. So every morning I say Kitty Ford is a renowned author. This is what motivated me to get up off the couch (sort of speak) and start working on my dream. Again thank you Mr. Steve Harvey.

Thanks to my family for their love and support.
I send my love to Brother Eric and Sister Angela Baltimore, who has always shown me unconditional love. They are always there when I just needed a shoulder to lean on. Two people whom I could depend on in staying real with me. Never sugar coated anything and giving me the word for any situation I may be going through.

Last but definitely not least, My Family at Chosen Ministry. I often heard that one man's junk is another man's treasure. When I felt unwanted and unloved you embraced me with so much love and you except me with unconditional love. I am so thankful and so bless to have you Pastor Timothy and First Lady LaJuanda Sherfield for my spiritual guidance.

I love you all

Table of Contents

Introduction

"But my God shall supply all your needs according to his riches in glory by Christ Jesus." Philip 4:19
"Enter into his gates with thanksgiving and into his courts with praise: be thankful unto him, and bless his name." Ps 100:4

Psalms 100:4 gives you instruction on how to get into the Lord's presence. Being thankful letting God know that you have faith to believe he hears your prayers and will answer your request, doing this in His name. That He should be Glorified, him and him alone.

Before you begin, you would want to take with you your Bible, pen and paper, along with your list of prayer request. The reason you take these items with you the Lord gives us answers in different ways. Sometimes he will give us a scripture, sometimes he will speak something to us, and when this happens we need to write it down. For Satan comes quickly to take the word from your heart. *"And these are they by the wayside, where the word is sown; but when they have heard, Satan cometh immediately, and taketh away the word that was sown in their hearts." Mk. 4:15*

The Lord does answers prayers immediately, however there are times he may take a day, a week, maybe a month or longer. This does not mean the he do not hear you. Sometimes he says yes, sometimes he says no, when he says no that is because he has something better for you. Then there are times he just says wait. While waiting on God be of good cheer.

"Be careful for nothing; but in everything by prayer and supplication with thanksgiving let you request be known unto God." Philip 4:6 (Careful here signifies anxious)

Wait on the Lord! God knows what you need even before you ask of it.

"Be not ye therefore like unto them: for Father knoweth what things *ye have need have before ye ask him." Matt 6:8*

When you pray, pray in faith, believing whatever you have petitioned, it shall come to pass. It is your faith that pleases God.

"But without faith it is impossible to please him: for he that cometh to God must believe that he is. And that he is a rewarder to them that diligently seek him." Hebrew 11:6

This One on One with the Master will give you a closer relationship with the Lord. This will allow you to spend quite time just you and him. Take at least thirty minutes daily use this time to learn of him, his nature, the way he shows love, the way he loves you. This will be an opportunity to show him love in return. Keep in mind that every time we go before Our Father we do not need to ask for anything. Remember not to take even the little things for granted. There are times when the only thing required is just saying Lord I thank you, and begin to worship Him.

I pray this will help to elevate you to a higher level in Christ Jesus!

Using the One on One with the Master

One on One with the Master is a personal Bible study.

2Tim.2:15 say to "Study to shew thyself approved unto God, a workman that needeth not to be ashamed, rightly dividing the word of truth." Therefore God has given us the Bible.

You will get to know God on a personal level; you will get to know him and doing His will.

This is why I believe devotional bible study is most important. In devotional bible study we are reading and studying His word in order that we may hear His voice, that we may know how to do His will and live a better Christian life.

How to use the One on One is a daily devotion, a tool for growth and Bible study.

1. Begin your daily devotion with prayer, asking God to open your eyes, your heart, and your mind that you might receive his word, and get true understanding.

2. Read the scriptures that are there, however it is always good to read the entire chapter or possible one or two verses before or after.

3. After reading ask yourself what this passage is saying to you, and then reread it.

4. Ask yourself these questions:

    a. What is the main subject or message?

    b. What does the passage teach me about the Lord Jesus Christ?

    c. Does the passage portray any sins for me to confess and forsake?

    d. Are there any promises for me to claim?

    e. Are there any instructions for me to follow?

    (Remember to take a pen and pad with you.)

5. Memorize passages of the Bible.

Pray when closing your devotion. Include in your prayer things that are listed in your prayer request section. Keep in mind that some prayers are answered right away, some prayers may be later. Just know that God is an on time God. He may not come when you want him, but he is always on time.

This daily devotion will give you a closer relationship with the Lord. This will allow you to spend quite time just you and him. Take at least thirty minutes to a hour daily use this time to learn of him, his nature, the way he shows love, the way he show you how to love others as he loves you. This will be an opportunity to show him love in return. Keep in mind that every time we go before Our Father we do not need to ask for anything. Remember not to take even the littlest things for granted. There are times when the only thing required is just saying Lord I thank you, and begin to worship Him.

I pray that this will be a tool for you to grow in the Word of God. For some it will help you to get connected to the vine. For others it will help you stay connected.

Overview of the Bible

The Holy Bible consists of sixty-six books. These books are divided into two (2) main sections The Old Testament and the New Testament. The Old Testament has 39 books the New Testament has 27 books. In the Old Testament we lived by law, in the New Testament we live by grace. Testament means covenant or an agreement. Both covenants are sealed by blood and mediated by man.

The Old Testament breakdown

There are five (5) books written by Moses known as the books of law also called the books of "Pentateuch."

Genesis

Exodus

Leviticus

Numbers

Deuteronomy

There are twelve (12) books called the *History books.*

Joshua	2nd King
Judges	1st Chronicles
Ruth	2nd Chronicles
1st Samuel	Ezra
2nd Samuel	Nehemiah
1st King	Esther

There are three (3) books called the *Books of Wisdom.*

Job

Proverbs

Ecclesiastes

There are three (3) books called the *Books of Poetry.*

Psalms

Songs of Solomon

Lamentation

There are sixteen (16) books called the *prophetic* books.

Isaiah	Jonah
Jeremiah	Micah
Ezekiel	Nahum
Daniel	Habakkuk
Hosea	Zephaniah
Joel	Haggai
Amos	Zechariah
Obadiah	Malachi

Breakdown of the New Testament

There are four (4) books in the New Testament called the *Gospel.*

Matthew

Mark

Luke

John

These four books along with the book of Acts are also called in the New Testament *History books.*

There are twenty-one (21) books called *letters or "epistles." This is* a form of writing among the ancient Greek.

Romans	Titus
1st Corinthians	Philemon
2nd Corinthians	Hebrew
Galatians	James
Ephesians	1st Peter
Philippians	2nd Peter
Colossians	1 John
1st Thessalonians	2 John
2nd Thessalonians	3 John
1st Timothy	Jude
2nd Timothy	

The *Apocalyptic book* is the book of Revelation.

Books of the Bible and Abbreviations

Old Testament

Gen....Genesis
Ex....Exodus
Lev...Leviticus
Num...Numbers
Deut...Deuteronomy
Josh...Joshua
Judg...Judges
Ruth...Ruth
1 Sam...1 Samuel
2 Sam...2 Samuel
1 Kin...1 Kings
2 Kin...2 Kings
1Chr...1 Chronicles
2 Chr....2Chronicles
Ezra...Ezra
Neh....Nehemiah
Esth....Esther
Job....Job
Ps....Psalms
Prov....Proverbs
Eccl....Ecclesiastes
Song ...Song of Solomon
Is....Isaiah
Jer....Jeremiah
Lam....Lamentations
Ezek...Ezekiel
Dan...Daniel
Hos....Hosea
Joel...Joel
Amos...Amos
Obad....Obadiah
Jon.....Jonah
Mic...Micah

Nah...Nahum
Hab....Habakkuk
Zeph...Zephaniah
Hag....Haggai
Zech...Zechariah
Mal....Malachi

New Testament

Mt....Matthew
Mk....Mark
Lk....Luke
Jn....John
Acts...Acts
Rom....Romans
1Cor...1Corinthians
2Cor...2Corinthians
Gal....Galatians
Eph....Ephesians
Phil....Philippians
Col....Colossians
1Thess...1Thessalonians
2Thess...2Thessalonians
1Tim…1Timothy
2Tim...2Timothy
Titus...Titus
Philem...Philemon
Heb...Hebrew
Jas...James
1Pet...1Peter
2Pet...2Peter
1Jn...1John
2Jn...2John
3Jn…3John
Jude...Jude
Rev...Revelation

Other Names and Titles of God
with Reference

ELOHIM meaning the Creator, it appears 2,700 times in the Bible. He relates to mankind as His creatures. *"Elohim is God the Son, the living "Word"* with creature form to create (John 1:1 Col. 1:15-17 Rev 3:14); and later, with human form to redeem (John 1:14).

JEHOVAH while Elohim is God as the Creator of all things, Jehovah is the same God in covenant relation to those whom He created. *Jehovah* means the Eternal, the Immutable One, He Who WAS, and IS and IS TO COME. Gen. 21:33. He is the God of Israel; and the God of those who are redeemed, and are thus now "in Christ". The name Jehovah is combined with ten other words, which form what are known as "the Jehovah Titles." These titles may be found in the Hebrew Canon, in the order in which they occur.

1. JEHOVAH-JIREH Jehovah will see, or provide. (Gen. 22:14)
2. JEHOVAH-ROPHEKA Jehovah that healeth thee. (Ex 15:26)
3. JEHOVAH-NISSI Jehovah my banner. (Ex 17:15)
4. JEHOVAH-MEKADDISHKEM Jehovah that doth sanctify you. (Ex 31:13; Lev 20:8; 21:8; 22:32)
5. JEHOVAH-SHALOM Jehovah sends peace. (Judge 6:24)
6. JEHOVAH-ZEBA'OTH Jehovah is host. (1Sam 1:3)
7. JEHOVAH-ZIDKENU Jehovah our righteousness. (Jer23: 6 & 33:16)
8. JEHOVAH-SHAMMAH Jehovah is there. (Ezek 48:35)
9. JEHOVAH-'ELYON Jehovah most high. (Ps 7: 17, 47:2 & 97:9)
10. JEHOVAH-RO'I Jehovah my Shepherd. (Ps 23: 1)

Other Names for Jesus

Advocate 1John 2:1
Almighty... Rev. 19:15
Alpha and Omega Rev.21:6
Author and finisher of our faith........ Heb.3:1
Beginning and the end .... Rev. 21:6
Beloved Eph.1:6
Bread of life..................................... John 6:35
Bridegroom .... John 3:29
Bright morning star.......................... Rev. 22:16
Chief corner stone .... Ps 118:22; Mark 12:10
Chosen of God................................. 1Pet. 2:4
Christ, the... John 1:41; Acts 9:22
Christ, Jesus .... Rom. 8:39
Counselor.. Is. 9:6
Emmanuel.. Matt. 1:23
Everlasting Father.............................. Is. 9:6
Faithful and true .... Rev. 19:11
Holy One 1John 2:20
Horn of salvation.............................. Luke 1:69
I Am .... John 8:58
Jesus.. Luke 1:31
Jesus Christ .... Rom 1:4
Jesus Christ our Lord .... Rom. 6:23
Jesus Christ our Savior .... Titus 3:6
Jesus of Nazareth.............................. Luke 24:19
Jesus, the Son of God .... Heb. 4:14
King of Kings.................................... 1Tim. 6:15
Lamb of God .... John 1:36
Light .... John 1:9
Light of the World............................ John 9:5
Living bread .... John 6:51
Lord .... John 21:7
Lord God Almighty .... Rev. 4:8
Lord and Savior Jesus Christ 2Pet. 2:20

Master... Mark 12:14
Mediator .... Heb. 12:24
Messiah... John 4:25, 26
Morning Star .... Rev. 22:6
Redeemer .... Is. 59:20
Righteous One .... Is 53:11
Rock 1Cor. 10:4
Rose of Sharon .... Song 2:1
Savior 1Tim. 4:10
Savior, Jesus Christ.......................... 2Pet. 2:20
Shepherd .... John 10:11
Son of God...................................... Rom. 1:4
Son of Man .... Acts 7:14
Son of the Father............................. 2 John 3
Son of the Most High .... Luke 1:32
True vine... John 15:1
Truth .... John 14:6
Way... John 14:6
Wonderful....................................... Is 9:6
Word... 1John 1:1
Word of Life.................................... 1John 1:1

Do not be fooled in order to see the Kingdom of God a sinner must be born again. John 3:3 says. Jesus answered and said unto him, verily, verily I say unto thee. Except a man be born again, he cannot see the kingdom of God.

Before beginning this daily devotion I would like to take the time to invite you to come to Christ if you have not already done so.

God wants you to know that you do not have to be in a church or in a large crowd of people to confess salvation (to be saved). You can be saved today, right at this moment. Salvation is between you and God, and He has provided us with a plan of salvation. *Roman 10:9* says "that if thou shall confess with thy mouth the Lord Jesus and shalt believe in thine heart that God hath raised him from the dead, thou shall be saved."

Do you believe that Jesus is Lord? Do you believe in your heart that he died and on the third day God raised him from the dead? If you said yes to these questions then you are saved.

You are now saved. In *Romans10: 10* it explains" For with your heart man believth unto righteousness and with the mouth confession is made unto salvation."

Welcome to the family. The question might be raised what family? You now belong to the family of righteousness, where our Father which is in heaven.

I urge you now to find a church to attend for *Acts 11:26* they assembled themselves with the church, and taught much people. And the disciples were called Christians. In search of a church, seek a church that is living the word (therefore you must study and read the word for yourself), a church that are not just hearers but doers of the word. A faith believing church; "For it is impossible to please God without faith",

A church that believe in true deliverance; a church that knows if you are sick in your body that God can and will heal you. Believing that the poor do not have to be poor anymore; that he can deliver a family member or even a friend from drugs, alcohol, and prostitution anything that is hindering them from accepting Our Lord and Savior; A church where the Holy Spirit is allowed to be in control. I belong to Chosen Ministries located in King George VA. Where the Spirit of the Lord is free

God has called His church into a life of ministry not as a part time endeavor but a full time work.

We at Chosen Ministries extend a hearty welcome to you and your family to join us as we reach for Gods best through Christ Jesus.

The daily devotion is for 365 days everyday of the year. You will have a scripture to read a key thought for that scripture, your thought on the scripture, your prayer request and the date your prayer was answer. Keep in mind your prayer could be answered before you finish your days devotion, it also may not come right away however if you keep the faith and believe that it is going to happen then it is.

Daily Devotion

DATE_____

DAY 1

For we are made partakers of Christ, if we hold the beginning of our confidence steadfast unto the end; *Heb. 3:14*

Key thought: Be faithful to the end.

YOUR KEY
THOUGHT: _____
_____
_____
_____

YOUR PRAYER
REQUEST: _____
_____
_____
_____
_____
_____
_____
_____

DATES PRAYERS
ANSWERED: _____
_____
_____
_____

DAY 2

The LORD will give strength unto his people; the Lord will bless his people with peace *Ps.29: 11*

Key Thought: with the Lord, there is peace.

YOUR KEY
THOUGHT: _____
_____
_____
_____

YOUR PRAYER
REQUEST: _____
_____
_____
_____
_____
_____
_____
_____

DATES PRAYERS
ANSWERED: _____
_____
_____
_____

DAY 3

The young lions do lack and suffer hunger; but they that seek the LORD shall not want any good thing. *Ps. 34:10*

Key Thought: You will never be in lack of any good thing.

YOUR KEY
THOUGHT: _____
_____
_____
_____

YOUR PRAYER
REQUEST: _____
_____
_____
_____
_____
_____
_____
_____

DATES PRAYERS
ANSWERED: _____
_____
_____
_____

DAY 4

Let all bitterness, and wrath, and anger, and clamour, and evil speaking, be put away from you with all malice *Eph. 4:31*

Key Thought: Get rid of malicious behavior.

YOUR KEY
THOUGHT: _____
_____
_____
_____

YOUR PRAYER
REQUEST: _____
_____
_____
_____
_____
_____
_____
_____

DATES PRAYERS
ANSWERED: _____
_____
_____
_____

DAY 5

Be not wise in thine own eyes; fear the LORD and depart from evil. *Prov.3: 7*

Key Thought: Do not be vain

YOUR KEY
THOUGHT: _____
_____
_____
_____

YOUR PRAYER
REQUEST: _____
_____
_____
_____
_____
_____
_____
_____

DATES PRAYERS
ANSWERED: _____
_____
_____
_____

DAY 6

But the fruit of the Spirit is love, joy, peace, longsuffering, gentleness, goodness, faith. *Gal. 5:22*

Key Thought: Live by the fruits of the Spirit.

YOUR KEY
THOUGHT: _____
_____
_____
_____

YOUR PRAYER
REQUEST: _____
_____
_____
_____
_____
_____
_____
_____
_____

DATES PRAYERS
ANSWERED: _____
_____
_____
_____

DAY 7

And God is able to make all grace abound toward you; that ye, always having all suffering in all things. may abound to every good works. *2Cor.9:8*

Key Thought: God is sufficient.

YOUR KEY
THOUGHT: _____
_____
_____
_____

YOUR PRAYER
REQUEST: _____
_____
_____
_____
_____
_____
_____
_____

DATES PRAYERS
ANSWERED: _____
_____
_____
_____

DAY 8

And the LORD shall guide thee continually and satisfy thy soul in drought, and make fat thy bones; and thou shalt he like a watered garden and like a spring of water, whose water fail not. *Is. 58:11*

Key Thought: The Lord will provide

YOUR KEY
THOUGHT: _____
_____
_____
_____

YOUR PRAYER
REQUEST: _____
_____
_____
_____
_____
_____
_____
_____

DATES PRAYERS
ANSWERED: _____
_____
_____
_____

DAY 9

In the beginning God created the heaven and earth. *Gen. 1:1*

Key Thought: God is our creator

YOUR KEY
THOUGHT: _____
_____
_____
_____

YOUR PRAYER
REQUEST: _____
_____
_____
_____
_____
_____
_____
_____

DATES PRAYERS
ANSWERED: _____
_____
_____
_____

DAY 10

For the LORD God is a sun and shield, the LORD will give grace and glory, no good thing will be with held from them that walk uprightly. *Ps. 84:11*

Key Thought: The Lord provides for all that walks upright.

YOUR KEY
THOUGHT: _____

_____

_____

_____

YOUR PRAYER
REQUEST: _____

_____

_____

_____

_____

_____

_____

_____

DATES PRAYERS
ANSWERED: _____

_____

_____

_____

DAY 11

And he is before all things, and by him all things consist. *Col. 1:17*

Key thought: In Christ Jesus all things consist.

YOUR KEY
THOUGHT: _____

_____

_____

_____

YOUR PRAYER
REQUEST: _____

_____

_____

_____

_____

_____

_____

_____

DATES PRAYERS
ANSWERED: _____

_____

_____

_____

DAY 12

For God has not given us the spirit of fear; but of power and of love and of a sound mind. *2Tim. 1:7*

Key Thought: God has not given us the spirit of fear.

YOUR KEY
THOUGHT: _____
_____
_____
_____

YOUR PRAYER
REQUEST: _____
_____
_____
_____
_____
_____
_____
_____

DATES PRAYERS
ANSWERED: _____
_____
_____
_____

DAY 13

What shall we then say to these things? If God be for us, who can be against us? *Rom. 8:31*

Key Thought: If God be for you, who can be against you?

YOUR KEY
THOUGHT: _____

_____

_____

_____

YOUR PRAYER
REQUEST: _____

_____

_____

_____

_____

_____

_____

_____

DATES PRAYERS
ANSWERED: _____

_____

_____

_____

DAY 14

In God have I put my trust, I will not be afraid what man can do unto me. *Ps.56:11*

Key Thought: In God I trust.

YOUR KEY
THOUGHT: _____
_____
_____
_____

YOUR PRAYER
REQUEST: _____
_____
_____
_____
_____
_____
_____
_____

DATES PRAYERS
ANSWERED: _____
_____
_____
_____

DAY 15

If we suffer, we shall also resign with him, if we deny him, he also will deny us. *2Tim. 2:12*

Key Thought: If we suffer, we will always resign.

YOUR KEY
THOUGHT: _____
_____
_____
_____

YOUR PRAYER
REQUEST: _____
_____
_____
_____
_____
_____
_____
_____

DATES PRAYERS
ANSWERED: _____
_____
_____
_____

DAY 16

For I delivered unto you first of all that which I also received, now that Christ died for our sins according to the scriptures. *1Cor. 15:3*

Key Thought: Christ died for our sins.

YOUR KEY
THOUGHT: _____
_____
_____
_____

YOUR PRAYER
REQUEST: _____
_____
_____
_____
_____
_____
_____
_____

DATES PRAYERS
ANSWERED: _____
_____
_____
_____

DAY 17

Not unto us, o LORD not unto us, but unto thy name give glory, for thy mercy, and for thy truth's sake. *Ps.115:3*

Key Thought: Give God the glory for all things.

YOUR KEY
THOUGHT: _____
_____
_____
_____

YOUR PRAYER
REQUEST: _____
_____
_____
_____
_____
_____
_____
_____

DATES PRAYERS
ANSWERED: _____
_____
_____
_____

DAY 18

And be not drunk with wine where in is excess, but be filled with the Spirit. *Eph.5:18*

Key Thought: Do not be drunk with wine but be drunk in the Spirit.

YOUR KEY
THOUGHT: _____

_____

_____

_____

YOUR PRAYER
REQUEST: _____

_____

_____

_____

_____

_____

_____

_____

DATES PRAYERS
ANSWERED: _____

_____

_____

_____

DAY 19

FOR HE THAT WILL LOVE LIFE, AND SEE GOOD DAYS, LET HIM REFRAIN HIS TONGUE FROM EVIL, AND HIS LIPS THAT THEY SPEAK NO GUILE. (deceit) *1Pet.3:10*

Key Thought: Do not gossip.

YOUR KEY
THOUGHT: _____
_____
_____
_____

YOUR PRAYER
REQUEST: _____
_____
_____
_____
_____
_____
_____
_____

DATES PRAYERS
ANSWERED: _____
_____
_____
_____

DAY 20

And if it seem evil unto you to serve the LORD, choose you this day whom ye will serve; whether the gods which your fathers served that were on the other side of the flood, or the gods of the Amorites, in whose land ye dwell, but as for me and my house, we will serve the LORD. *Josh. 24:15*

Key Thought: Choose the Lord today.

YOUR KEY
THOUGHT: _____
_____
_____
_____

YOUR PRAYER
REQUEST: _____
_____
_____
_____
_____
_____
_____
_____

DATES PRAYERS
ANSWERED: _____
_____
_____
_____

DAY 21

In the last day, that great day of the feast, Jesus stood and cried saying, If any man thirst, let him come unto me, and drink. *Jn.7:37*

Key Thought: Seek Jesus for the answer.

YOUR KEY
THOUGHT: _____
_____
_____
_____

YOUR PRAYER
REQUEST: _____
_____
_____
_____
_____
_____
_____
_____

DATES PRAYERS
ANSWERED: _____
_____
_____
_____

DAY 22

Then Peter and the other apostles answered and said, We ought to obey God rather than man. *Acts 5:29*

Key Thought: Obey God rather than man.

YOUR KEY
THOUGHT: _____
_____
_____
_____

YOUR PRAYER
REQUEST: _____
_____
_____
_____
_____
_____
_____
_____

DATES PRAYERS
ANSWERED: _____
_____
_____
_____

DAY 23

And ye shall seek me, and find me, when ye shall search for me with all your heart. *Jerm.29:13*

Key Thought: Seek God with your heart not your lips.

YOUR KEY
THOUGHT: _____
_____
_____
_____

YOUR PRAYER
REQUEST: _____
_____
_____
_____
_____
_____
_____
_____

DATES PRAYERS
ANSWERED: _____
_____
_____
_____

DAY 24

I can do all things through Christ which strengtheneth me. *Phil.4:13*

Key Thought: You can do all things through Christ.

YOUR KEY
THOUGHT: _____
_____
_____
_____

YOUR PRAYER
REQUEST: _____
_____
_____
_____
_____
_____
_____
_____
_____

DATES PRAYERS
ANSWERED: _____
_____
_____
_____

DATE_____

DAY 25

The women shall not wear that which pertaineth unto man, neither shall a man put on a woman's garment: for all that do so are abomination unto the LORD thy God. *Deut. 22:5*

Key Thought: God do not accept cross dressing.

YOUR KEY
THOUGHT: _____
_____
_____
_____

YOUR PRAYER
REQUEST: _____
_____
_____
_____
_____
_____
_____
_____

DATES PRAYERS
ANSWERED: _____
_____
_____
_____

DATE_____

DAY 26
Before I formed thee in the belly I knew thee; and before thou camest forth out of the womb I sanctified thee, and I ordained thee a prophet unto the nation. *Jerm. 1:5*

Key Thought: God has a purpose for us all while we were yet in our mothers womb.

YOUR KEY
THOUGHT: _____
_____
_____
_____

YOUR PRAYER
REQUEST: _____
_____
_____
_____
_____
_____
_____
_____

DATES PRAYERS
ANSWERED: _____
_____
_____
_____

DAY 27

But he said unto her, thou speakest as one of the foolish women speaketh. What? shall we receive good at the hand of God, and shall we not receive evil? In all this do not Job sin with his lips. *Job 1:10*

Key Thought: Accept God <u>allows</u> good and adversities in your life.

YOUR KEY
THOUGHT: _____
_____
_____
_____

YOUR PRAYER
REQUEST: _____
_____
_____
_____
_____
_____
_____
_____

DATES PRAYERS
ANSWERED: _____
_____
_____
_____

DATE_____

DAY 28
That the beginning of Abraham might come on the Gentiles through Jesus Christ; that we might receive the promise of the Spirit through faith. *Gal. 3:26*

Key Thought: Adopted into God's family by faith in Jesus Christ.

YOUR KEY
THOUGHT: _____
_____
_____
_____

YOUR PRAYER
REQUEST: _____
_____
_____
_____
_____
_____
_____
_____

DATES PRAYERS
ANSWERED: _____
_____
_____
_____

DAY 29

But that we write unto them that they abstain from pollution of idols, and from fornication, and from things strangled, and from blood. *Acts 15:20*

Key Thought: Abstain from sexual immorality.

YOUR KEY
THOUGHT: _____
_____
_____
_____

YOUR PRAYER
REQUEST: _____
_____
_____
_____
_____
_____
_____
_____

DATES PRAYERS
ANSWERED: _____
_____
_____
_____

DAY 30

Yet man is born unto trouble as the sparks fly upward. *Job 5:7*

Key Thought: Everyone encounters trouble.

YOUR KEY
THOUGHT: _____
_____
_____
_____

YOUR PRAYER
REQUEST: _____
_____
_____
_____
_____
_____
_____
_____

DATES PRAYERS
ANSWERED: _____
_____
_____
_____

DAY 31

Let us therefore come boldly unto the throne of grace, that we may obtain mercy and find grace to help in time of need. *Heb. 4:16*

Key Thought: Go before the Lord boldly.

YOUR KEY
THOUGHT: _____
_____
_____
_____

YOUR PRAYER
REQUEST: _____
_____
_____
_____
_____
_____
_____
_____

DATES PRAYERS
ANSWERED: _____
_____
_____
_____

DAY 32
Wherefore my beloved brethren, let every man be swift to hear, slow to speak, slow to wrath.
Jas.1:19

Key Thought: Be quick to hear what God is saying to you.

YOUR KEY
THOUGHT: _____
_____
_____
_____

YOUR PRAYER
REQUEST: _____
_____
_____
_____
_____
_____
_____
_____
_____

DATES PRAYERS
ANSWERED: _____
_____
_____
_____

DAY 33

I am the vine, ye are the branches: He that abideth in me, and I in him, the same bringeth forth much fruit: for without me ye can do nothing. *Jn.15:7*

Key Thought: Apart from Christ you can do nothing.

YOUR KEY
THOUGHT: _____
_____
_____
_____

YOUR PRAYER
REQUEST: _____
_____
_____
_____
_____
_____
_____
_____

DATES PRAYERS
ANSWERED: _____
_____
_____
_____

DAY 34

My son, hear the instruction of thy father, and forsake not the law of thy mother. *Prov. 1:8*

Key Thought: Obey your parents

YOUR KEY
THOUGHT: _____
_____
_____
_____

YOUR PRAYER
REQUEST: _____
_____
_____
_____
_____
_____
_____
_____

DATES PRAYERS
ANSWERED: _____
_____
_____
_____

DAY 35

Lay not up for yourself treasures upon earth, where moth and rust doth corrupt, and where thieves break through and steal. *Matt. 6:19*

Key Thought: Do not stow up treasures here on earth.

YOUR KEY
THOUGHT: _____
_____
_____
_____

YOUR PRAYER
REQUEST: _____
_____
_____
_____
_____
_____
_____
_____

DATES PRAYERS
ANSWERED: _____
_____
_____
_____

DAY 36

It is good neither to eat flesh, nor to drink wine, nor any thing whereby thy brother stumbleth, or is offended, or is made weak. *Rom. 14:21*

Key Thought: Cause not your brother to stumble.

YOUR KEY
THOUGHT: _____
_____
_____
_____

YOUR PRAYER
REQUEST: _____
_____
_____
_____
_____
_____
_____
_____

DATES PRAYERS
ANSWERED: _____
_____
_____
_____

DAY 37

But to do good and to communicate forget not: for with such sacrifices God is well pleased. *Heb. 13:16*

Key Thought: God is well pleased with doing good, and sacrifices.

YOUR KEY
THOUGHT: _____
_____
_____
_____

YOUR PRAYER
REQUEST: _____
_____
_____
_____
_____
_____
_____
_____

DATES PRAYERS
ANSWERED: _____
_____
_____
_____

DAY 38

For what is a man profited, if he shall gain the whole world, and lose his own soul? *Matt.16:26*

Key Thought: Is it worth gaining the world and losing your soul?

YOUR KEY
THOUGHT: _____

_____
_____
_____

YOUR PRAYER
REQUEST: _____

_____
_____
_____
_____
_____
_____
_____

DATES PRAYERS
ANSWERED: _____

_____
_____
_____

DAY 39

Thou lovest righteousness, and hatest wickedness; therefore God, thy God hath anointed thee with the oil of gladness above thy fellows. *Ps. 45:7*

Key Thought: God anoints with oil of joy.

YOUR KEY
THOUGHT: _____
_____
_____
_____

YOUR PRAYER
REQUEST: _____
_____
_____
_____
_____
_____
_____
_____

DATES PRAYERS
ANSWERED: _____
_____
_____
_____

DAY 40

When my mother and my father forsake me; then the LORD will take me up. *Ps. 27:10*

Key Thought: Even if your parents forsake you, the Lord will not.

YOUR KEY
THOUGHT: _____

_____
_____
_____

YOUR PRAYER
REQUEST: _____

_____
_____
_____
_____
_____
_____
_____

DATES PRAYERS
ANSWERED: _____

_____
_____
_____

DAY 41

And the LORD, he it is that doth go before thee; he will be with thee; he will not fail thee, neither forsake thee; fear not, neither be dismayed. *Deut. 31:8*

Key Thought: God will not forsake you in the time of need.

YOUR KEY
THOUGHT: _____
_____
_____
_____

YOUR PRAYER
REQUEST: _____
_____
_____
_____
_____
_____
_____
_____

DATES PRAYERS
ANSWERED: _____
_____
_____
_____

DAY 42

Divers weight are an abomination unto the LORD, and a false balance is not good.
Prov. 20:23

Key Thought: Dishonesty is an abomination of God.

YOUR KEY
THOUGHT: _____
_____
_____
_____

YOUR PRAYER
REQUEST: _____
_____
_____
_____
_____
_____
_____
_____

DATES PRAYERS
ANSWERED: _____
_____
_____
_____

DAY 43

All things were made by him; and without him was not anything made that was made.
Jn. 1:3

Key Thought: All things are created by Christ.

YOUR KEY
THOUGHT: _____
_____
_____
_____

YOUR PRAYER
REQUEST: _____
_____
_____
_____
_____
_____
_____
_____

DATES PRAYERS
ANSWERED: _____
_____
_____
_____

DAY 44

And David danced before the LORD with all his might and David was girded with a linen e'-phod. *2 Sam. 6:14*

Key Thought: David danced before the Lord.

YOUR KEY
THOUGHT: _____
_____
_____
_____

YOUR PRAYER
REQUEST: _____
_____
_____
_____
_____
_____
_____
_____

DATES PRAYERS
ANSWERED: _____
_____
_____
_____

DAY 45

And Jesus said unto him verily I say unto thee, to day shalt thou be with me in paradise. *Lk. 23:43*

Key Thought: Believers go to be with the Lord.

YOUR KEY
THOUGHT: _____
_____
_____
_____

YOUR PRAYER
REQUEST: _____
_____
_____
_____
_____
_____
_____
_____

DATES PRAYERS
ANSWERED: _____
_____
_____
_____

DAY 46

Blessed is the man whom thou chastenest, O LORD, and teachest him out of thy law. *Ps. 94:12*

Key Thought: Blessed are those God corrects.

YOUR KEY
THOUGHT: _____
_____
_____
_____

YOUR PRAYER
REQUEST: _____
_____
_____
_____
_____
_____
_____
_____

DATES PRAYERS
ANSWERED: _____
_____
_____
_____

DAY 47

Thou shalt not defraud thy neighbors; neither rob him; the wages of him that is hired shall not abide with thee all night until the morning. *Lev.19:13*

Key Thought: Do not cheat anyone.

YOUR KEY
THOUGHT: _____
_____
_____
_____

YOUR PRAYER
REQUEST: _____
_____
_____
_____
_____
_____
_____
_____

DATES PRAYERS
ANSWERED: _____
_____
_____
_____

DAY 48

But be ye doers of the word, and not hearers only; deceiving your own self. *Jas. 1:22*

Key Thought: Be doers not just hearers of the word.

YOUR KEY
THOUGHT: _____
_____
_____
_____

YOUR PRAYER
REQUEST: _____
_____
_____
_____
_____
_____
_____
_____

DATES PRAYERS
ANSWERED: _____
_____
_____
_____

DAY 49

For whosoever shall do the will of my Father which is in heaven the same is my brother, and sister, and mother. *Matt. 12:50*

Key Thought: Doing Gods' will, puts you in Jesus family.

YOUR KEY
THOUGHT: _____
_____
_____
_____

YOUR PRAYER
REQUEST: _____
_____
_____
_____
_____
_____
_____
_____

DATES PRAYERS
ANSWERED: _____
_____
_____
_____

DAY 50

And Jesus said unto them. Because of your unbelief; for verily I say unto you, If you have faith as a grain of a mustard seed, ye shall say unto the mountain, Remove hence to yonder place; and it shall remove; and nothing shall be impossible unto you. *Matt: 17:20*

Key Thought: Small faith can bring large miracles.

YOUR KEY
THOUGHT: _____
_____
_____
_____

YOUR PRAYER
REQUEST: _____
_____
_____
_____
_____
_____
_____
_____

DATES PRAYERS
ANSWERED: _____
_____
_____
_____

DAY 51

Whose adorning let it not be that outward adorning of plating the hair, and of wearing of gold, or of putting on of apparel; But let it be the hidden man of the heart, in which is not corruptible, *even the ornaments* of a meek and quiet spirit, which is in the sight of God of great price. *1 Pet. 3: 3-4*

Key Thought: Be not so overly concerned about the outer appearance for God looks at the heart of man, and reward you accordingly.

YOUR KEY
THOUGHT: _____
_____
_____
_____

YOUR PRAYER
REQUEST: _____
_____
_____
_____
_____
_____
_____
_____

DATES PRAYERS
ANSWERED: _____
_____
_____
_____

DAY 52

For the love of money is the most of all evil; which while some coveted after, they have erred from the faith; and pierced themselves through with many sorrows. *1Tim.6:10*

Key Thought: Avoid the love of money.

YOUR KEY
THOUGHT: _____
_____
_____
_____

YOUR PRAYER
REQUEST: _____
_____
_____
_____
_____
_____
_____
_____

DATES PRAYERS
ANSWERED: _____
_____
_____
_____

DAY 53

But the comforter, which is the Holy Ghost, whom the Father will send in my name, he shall teach you all things; and bring all things to your remembrance, whatsoever I have said unto you. *Jn. 14:26*

Key Thought: The Holy Ghost will teach you and bring all things back to your remembrance.

YOUR KEY
THOUGHT: _____

_____

_____

_____

YOUR PRAYER
REQUEST: _____

_____

_____

_____

_____

_____

_____

_____

DATES PRAYERS
ANSWERED: _____

_____

_____

_____

DAY 54

According as he hath chosen us in him before the foundation of the world, that we should be holy and without blame before in love: *Eph. 1:4*

Key Thought: You are chosen in Christ.

YOUR KEY
THOUGHT: _____
_____
_____
_____

YOUR PRAYER
REQUEST: _____
_____
_____
_____
_____
_____
_____
_____

DATES PRAYERS
ANSWERED: _____
_____
_____
_____

DAY 55

No man can come to me; except the Father which hath sent me draw him: and I will raise him up at the last day. *Jn. 6:44*

Key Thought: The Father in heaven draws you to Christ.

YOUR KEY
THOUGHT: _____
_____
_____
_____

YOUR PRAYER
REQUEST: _____
_____
_____
_____
_____
_____
_____
_____

DATES PRAYERS
ANSWERED: _____
_____
_____
_____

DAY 56

That we should be to praise of his glory, who first trusted in Christ. *Eph. 1:12*

Key Thought: Praise God in His glory.

YOUR KEY
THOUGHT: _____
_____
_____
_____

YOUR PRAYER
REQUEST: _____
_____
_____
_____
_____
_____
_____
_____

DATES PRAYERS
ANSWERED: _____
_____
_____
_____

DAY 57

Thou lovest righteousness, and hatest wickedness; therefore God, thy God, hath anointed thee with oil of gladness above thy fellows. *Ps. 45:7*

Key Thought: God anoints with oil of joy.

YOUR KEY
THOUGHT: _____
_____
_____
_____

YOUR PRAYER
REQUEST: _____
_____
_____
_____
_____
_____
_____
_____

DATES PRAYERS
ANSWERED: _____
_____
_____
_____

DAY 58

And I give unto them eternal life; and they shall never perish, neither shall any man pluck them out of my hand. *Jn.10:28*

Key Thought: Believers shall never perish

YOUR KEY
THOUGHT: _____
_____
_____
_____

YOUR PRAYER
REQUEST: _____
_____
_____
_____
_____
_____
_____
_____

DATES PRAYERS
ANSWERED: _____
_____
_____
_____

DAY 59

And he said unto me; My grace is sufficient for thee: for my strength is made perfect in weakness. *2Cor.12:9*

Key Thought: Christ's strength is made perfect in weakness.

YOUR KEY
THOUGHT: _____

_____

_____

_____

YOUR PRAYER
REQUEST: _____

_____

_____

_____

_____

_____

_____

_____

DATES PRAYERS
ANSWERED: _____

_____

_____

_____

DAY 60

It is of the Lord's mercies that we are not consumed; because his compassion fail not. They are new every morning great is the faithfulness. *Lam. 3:22-23*

Key Thought: God blesses with new mercies every morning.

YOUR KEY
THOUGHT: _____
_____
_____
_____

YOUR PRAYER
REQUEST: _____
_____
_____
_____
_____
_____
_____
_____

DATES PRAYERS
ANSWERED: _____
_____
_____
_____

DAY 61
Blessed is the man that trusteth in the Lord, and whose hope the Lord is. *Jer.17:7*

Ke*y Thought:* Blessed are those who trust in the Lord.

YOUR KEY
THOUGHT: _____
_____
_____
_____

YOUR PRAYER
REQUEST: _____
_____
_____
_____
_____
_____
_____
_____

DATES PRAYERS
ANSWERED: _____
_____
_____
_____

DATE_____

DAY 62
Blessed is that man that maketh the LORD his trust, and respecteth not the proud, nor such as turn aside to lies. *Ps. 40:4*

Key Thought: Be not proud, nor be a liar.

YOUR KEY
THOUGHT: _____
_____
_____
_____

YOUR PRAYER
REQUEST: _____
_____
_____
_____
_____
_____
_____
_____

DATES PRAYERS
ANSWERED: _____
_____
_____
_____

DAY 63

For we walk by faith, not by sight. *2Cor.5:17*

Key Thought: Live by faith not by what we see.

YOUR KEY
THOUGHT: _____

_____

_____

_____

YOUR PRAYER
REQUEST: _____

_____

_____

_____

_____

_____

_____

_____

DATES PRAYERS
ANSWERED: _____

_____

_____

_____

DAY 64

He that is of a proud heart stirreth up strife; but he that putteth his trust in the Lord shall be made fat. *Prov. 28:25*

Key Thought: Trusting God leads us to prosperity.

YOUR KEY
THOUGHT: _____

_____

_____

_____

YOUR PRAYER
REQUEST: _____

_____

_____

_____

_____

_____

_____

_____

DATES PRAYERS
ANSWERED: _____

_____

_____

_____

DAY 65

He that trusteth in his own heart is a fool; but whoso walketh wisely, he shall be delivered.
Prov. 28:26

Key Thought: Trusting in self is foolish.

YOUR KEY
THOUGHT: _____
_____
_____
_____

YOUR PRAYER
REQUEST: _____
_____
_____
_____
_____
_____
_____
_____

DATES PRAYERS
ANSWERED: _____
_____
_____
_____

DAY 66

For ye have not received the spirit if bondage again to fear; but ye have received the Spirit of adoption; whereby we cry, Ab'-ba Father. *Roman 8:15*

Key Thought: Adoption into God's family.

YOUR KEY
THOUGHT: _____
_____
_____
_____

YOUR PRAYER
REQUEST: _____
_____
_____
_____
_____
_____
_____
_____
_____

DATES PRAYERS
ANSWERED: _____
_____
_____
_____

DAY 67

And the brother shall deliver up the brother to death, and the father the child, and the children shall rise up against their parents and cause them to be put to death. *Matt.10:21*

Key Thought: Family will betray you.

YOUR KEY
THOUGHT: _____
_____
_____
_____

YOUR PRAYER
REQUEST: _____
_____
_____
_____
_____
_____
_____
_____

DATES PRAYERS
ANSWERED: _____
_____
_____
_____

DAY 68

For out of the heart proceed evil thoughts, murders, adulteries, fornications, thefts, false witness, blasphemies. *Matt. 15:19*

Key Thought: Evil comes from the heart.

YOUR KEY
THOUGHT: _____
_____
_____
_____

YOUR PRAYER
REQUEST: _____
_____
_____
_____
_____
_____
_____
_____

DATES PRAYERS
ANSWERED: _____
_____
_____
_____

DAY 69

If any man come to me and hate not his father, and mother, and wife, and children, and brethren, and sisters, yea and his own life also, he cannot be my disciple. *Lk.14:26*

Key Thought: To be a disciple of Jesus family must be forsaken.

YOUR KEY
THOUGHT: _____
_____
_____
_____

YOUR PRAYER
REQUEST: _____
_____
_____
_____
_____
_____
_____
_____

DATES PRAYERS
ANSWERED: _____
_____
_____
_____

DATE_____

DAY 70
And call no man your father upon the earth; for one is your Father, which is in heaven. *Matt.23:9*

Key Thought: Do not address anyone Father that is on earth.

YOUR KEY
THOUGHT: _____
_____
_____
_____

YOUR PRAYER
REQUEST: _____
_____
_____
_____
_____
_____
_____
_____

DATES PRAYERS
ANSWERED: _____
_____
_____
_____

DAY 71

What shall we say to these things? If God be for us, who can be against? *Rom.8:31*

Key Thought: If God is for us, who can be against us?

YOUR KEY
THOUGHT: _____
_____
_____
_____

YOUR PRAYER
REQUEST: _____
_____
_____
_____
_____
_____
_____
_____

DATES PRAYERS
ANSWERED: _____
_____
_____
_____

DAY 72

Jesus said unto him, if thou wilt be perfect, go and sell that thou hast and give to the poor, and thou shall have treasure in heaven, and come and follow me. *Matt. 19:21*

Key Thought: In striving for perfection, sacrifice and give to the poor.

YOUR KEY
THOUGHT: _____
_____
_____
_____

YOUR PRAYER
REQUEST: _____
_____
_____
_____
_____
_____
_____
_____

DATES PRAYERS
ANSWERED: _____
_____
_____
_____

DAY 73

Fight the good fight of faith, lay hold on eternal life, whereunto thou art also called, and hast professed a good profession before many witnesses. *1Tim. 6:12*

Key Thought: Fight the good fight.

YOUR KEY
THOUGHT: _____
_____
_____
_____

YOUR PRAYER
REQUEST: _____
_____
_____
_____
_____
_____
_____
_____

DATES PRAYERS
ANSWERED: _____
_____
_____
_____

DAY 74

Will a man rob God? Yet ye have robbed me, but ye say, wherein have we robbed thee? In tithes and offering. *Mal. 3:8*

Key Thought: Pay tithes and offering.

YOUR KEY
THOUGHT: _____

_____

_____

_____

YOUR PRAYER
REQUEST: _____

_____

_____

_____

_____

_____

_____

_____

DATES PRAYERS
ANSWERED: _____

_____

_____

_____

DAY 75

Love ye therefore the stranger; for ye were strangers in the land of Egypt.
Deut. 10:19

Key Thought: show love to everyone, including strangers.

YOUR KEY
THOUGHT: _____
_____
_____
_____

YOUR PRAYER
REQUEST: _____
_____
_____
_____
_____
_____
_____
_____

DATES PRAYERS
ANSWERED: _____
_____
_____
_____

DAY 76

Then beware lest thou forget the LORD, which brought thee forth out of the land of Egypt, from the house of bondage. *Deut. 6:12*

Key Thought: Be careful not to forget the Lord our God, who delivered you from bondage.

YOUR KEY
THOUGHT: _____
_____
_____
_____

YOUR PRAYER
REQUEST: _____
_____
_____
_____
_____
_____
_____
_____

DATES PRAYERS
ANSWERED: _____
_____
_____
_____

DAY 77

Therefore hearken not ye to your prophets, nor to your divines, nor to your dreams, nor to your enchanters, nor to your sorcerers, which speak unto you saying, ye shall not serve the king of Babylon. *Jer.27*:9

Key Thought: Do not partake in fortune telling, and witchcraft.

YOUR KEY
THOUGHT: _____
_____
_____
_____

YOUR PRAYER
REQUEST: _____
_____
_____
_____
_____
_____
_____
_____

DATES PRAYERS
ANSWERED: _____
_____
_____
_____

DAY 78

Can two walk together unless they agree? *Amos 3:3*

Key Thought: How can two walk together unless they agree?

YOUR KEY
THOUGHT: _____
_____
_____
_____

YOUR PRAYER
REQUEST: _____
_____
_____
_____
_____
_____
_____
_____

DATES PRAYERS
ANSWERED: _____
_____
_____
_____

DAY 79

A friend loveth at all times, and a brother is born for adversity. *Prov.17:17*

Key Thought: A friend loves at all time.

YOUR KEY
THOUGHT: _____
_____
_____
_____

YOUR PRAYER
REQUEST: _____
_____
_____
_____
_____
_____
_____
_____

DATES PRAYERS
ANSWERED: _____
_____
_____
_____

DAY 80

A froward man soweth strife and a whisperer seperateth chief friends. *Prov.16:28*

Key Thought: Gossip will destroy friendship.

YOUR KEY
THOUGHT: _____
_____
_____
_____

YOUR PRAYER
REQUEST: _____
_____
_____
_____
_____
_____
_____
_____

DATES PRAYERS
ANSWERED: _____
_____
_____
_____

DAY 81

This spake he signifying by what death he should glorify God. And when he had spoken this, he saith unto him. Follow me. *John 21:19*

Key Thought: Glorify God even in death.

YOUR KEY
THOUGHT: _____
_____
_____
_____

YOUR PRAYER
REQUEST: _____
_____
_____
_____
_____
_____
_____
_____

DATES PRAYERS
ANSWERED: _____
_____
_____
_____

DAY 82

For he spake, and it was done; he commanded, and it stood fast. *Ps.33:9*

Key Thought: Whatever God says, will last.

YOUR KEY
THOUGHT: _____
_____
_____
_____

YOUR PRAYER
REQUEST: _____
_____
_____
_____
_____
_____
_____
_____

DATES PRAYERS
ANSWERED: _____
_____
_____
_____

DAY 83

In the day when God shall judge the secrets of men by Jesus Christ according to my gospel.
Rom. 2:16

Key Thought: According to the gospel of Jesus Christ, God will judge men's secrets.

YOUR KEY
THOUGHT: _____

_____

_____

_____

YOUR PRAYER
REQUEST: _____

_____

_____

_____

_____

_____

_____

DATES PRAYERS
ANSWERED: _____

_____

_____

_____

DAY 84

I am Alpha and Omega, the beginning and the ending, saith the Lord which is, and which was, and which is to come, the Almighty. *Rev. 1:8*

Key Thought: Jesus is Alpha and Omega, the beginning and the end.

YOUR KEY
THOUGHT: _____
_____
_____
_____

YOUR PRAYER
REQUEST: _____
_____
_____
_____
_____
_____
_____
_____

DATES PRAYERS
ANSWERED: _____
_____
_____
_____

DAY 85

Before the mountains were bought forth, or ever thou hadst formed the earth and the world, even from everlasting to everlasting, thou *art* God. *Ps.90:2*

Key Thought: God is from everlasting to everlasting.

YOUR KEY
THOUGHT: _____
_____
_____
_____

YOUR PRAYER
REQUEST: _____
_____
_____
_____
_____
_____
_____
_____

DATES PRAYERS
ANSWERED: _____
_____
_____
_____

DAY 86

Moreover the law entered, that the offence might abound. but where sin abounded grace did much more abound. *Rom.5:20*

Key Thought: Where sin increase, grace increased more.

YOUR KEY
THOUGHT: _____
_____
_____
_____

YOUR PRAYER
REQUEST: _____
_____
_____
_____
_____
_____
_____
_____

DATES PRAYERS
ANSWERED: _____
_____
_____
_____

DAY 87

For I am the LORD your God; ye shall therefore sanctify yourselves, and ye be holy; for I am holy; neither shall ye defile yourselves with any manner of creeping thing that creepeth upon the earth. *Lev.11:44*

Key Thought: Be holy for, God is holy.

YOUR KEY
THOUGHT: _____
_____
_____
_____

YOUR PRAYER
REQUEST: _____
_____
_____
_____
_____
_____
_____
_____

DATES PRAYERS
ANSWERED: _____
_____
_____
_____

DAY 88

For I am the LORD, I change not; therefore ye sons of Jacob are not consumed. *Mal. 3:6*

Key Thought: The Lord changes not.

YOUR KEY
THOUGHT: _____
_____
_____
_____

YOUR PRAYER
REQUEST: _____
_____
_____
_____
_____
_____
_____
_____

DATES PRAYERS
ANSWERED: _____
_____
_____
_____

DAY 89

Thou shalt not bow down thyself to them, nor serve them; for I the LORD thy God am a jealous God, visiting the iniquity of the fathers upon the children unto the third and fourth *generation* of them that hate me. *Ex.20:5*

Key Thought: Serve no other except He, for my God is a jealous God.

YOUR KEY
THOUGHT: _____
_____
_____
_____

YOUR PRAYER
REQUEST: _____
_____
_____
_____
_____
_____
_____
_____

DATES PRAYERS
ANSWERED: _____
_____
_____
_____

DAY 90

O give thanks unto the LORD; for he is good; for his mercy endureth forever. *1Chr.16:34*

Key Thought: The Lords mercy endureth forever.

YOUR KEY
THOUGHT: _____
_____
_____
_____

YOUR PRAYER
REQUEST: _____
_____
_____
_____
_____
_____
_____
_____

DATES PRAYERS
ANSWERED: _____
_____
_____
_____

DAY 91

But Jesus beheld them, and said unto them, with men this is impossible; but with God all things are possible. *Matt. 19:26*

Key Thought: With Jesus all things are possible.

YOUR KEY
THOUGHT: _____
_____
_____
_____

YOUR PRAYER
REQUEST: _____
_____
_____
_____
_____
_____
_____
_____

DATES PRAYERS
ANSWERED: _____
_____
_____
_____

DAY 92

Shall not God search this out? For he knoweth the secret of the heart. *Ps.44:21*

Key *Thought:* God knows the secrets of the heart.

YOUR KEY
THOUGHT: _____
_____
_____
_____

YOUR PRAYER
REQUEST: _____
_____
_____
_____
_____
_____
_____
_____
_____

DATES PRAYERS
ANSWERED: _____
_____
_____
_____

DAY 93

In God have I put my trust; I will not be afraid what man can do unto me. *Ps.56:11*

Key Thought: Put your trust in God.

YOUR KEY
THOUGHT: _____

_____

_____

_____

YOUR PRAYER
REQUEST: _____

_____

_____

_____

_____

_____

_____

_____

DATES PRAYERS
ANSWERED: _____

_____

_____

_____

DAY 94

For if our hearts condemn us God is greater then our heart, and knoweth all things. *1John 3:20*

Key Thought: There are no secrets from God.

YOUR KEY
THOUGHT: _____

_____

_____

_____

YOUR PRAYER
REQUEST: _____

_____

_____

_____

_____

_____

_____

_____

DATES PRAYERS
ANSWERED: _____

_____

_____

_____

DAY 95

The Lord is not slack concerning his promise, as some men count slackness; but is longsuffering to usward, not willing that any should perish, but that all should come to repentance. *2Pet.3:9*

Key Thought: God desire that no man shall perish.

YOUR KEY
THOUGHT: _____

_____

_____

_____

YOUR PRAYER
REQUEST: _____

_____

_____

_____

_____

_____

_____

_____

DATES PRAYERS
ANSWERED: _____

_____

_____

_____

DAY 96

And the LORD passed by before him, and proclaimed The LORD, The LORD GOD, merciful and gracious, longsuffering, and abundant to goodness and truth. *Ex. 34:6*

Key Thought: The Lord God is merciful and gracious.

YOUR KEY
THOUGHT: _____
_____
_____
_____

YOUR PRAYER
REQUEST: _____
_____
_____
_____
_____
_____
_____
_____

DATES PRAYERS
ANSWERED: _____
_____
_____
_____

DAY 97

For thus saith the high and lofty ONE that inhabiteth eternity, whose name is Holy; I dwell in the high and holy *place*, with him also *that is* of a contrite and humble spirit, and to revive the spirit of the humble, and to revive the heart of contrite ones. *Is.57:15*

Key Thought: God dwells with the humble.

YOUR KEY
THOUGHT: _____
_____
_____
_____

YOUR PRAYER
REQUEST: _____
_____
_____
_____
_____
_____
_____
_____

DATES PRAYERS
ANSWERED: _____
_____
_____
_____

DAY 98

I know that thou canst do everything, and that no thought can be withholden from thee.
Job 42:2

Key Thought: Whatever you thinketh God can do it.

YOUR KEY
THOUGHT: _____
_____
_____
_____

YOUR PRAYER
REQUEST: _____
_____
_____
_____
_____
_____
_____
_____

DATES PRAYERS
ANSWERED: _____
_____
_____
_____

DAY 99

There hath no temptation taken you but such as in common to man; but God is faithful, who with not suffer you to be tempted above that ye are able; but will with the temptation also make a way to escape, that ye may be able to bear it. 1Cor. 10:13

Key Thought: God has made a way to escape temptation.

YOUR KEY
THOUGHT: _____
_____
_____
_____

YOUR PRAYER
REQUEST: _____
_____
_____
_____
_____
_____
_____
_____

DATES PRAYERS
ANSWERED: _____
_____
_____
_____

DAY 100

Therefore all things whatsoever ye would that men should do to you, do ye even so to them; for this is the law and the prophets. *Matt.7:12*

Key Thought: Do unto others as you would have them to do unto you.

YOUR KEY
THOUGHT: _____
_____
_____
_____

YOUR PRAYER
REQUEST: _____
_____
_____
_____
_____
_____
_____
_____

DATES PRAYERS
ANSWERED: _____
_____
_____
_____

DAY 101

Thou shalt not avenge, nor bear any grudge against the children of thy people, but thou shalt love thy neighbor as thyself; I *am* the LORD. *Lev. 19:18*

Key Thought: Love your neighbor as yourself.

YOUR KEY
THOUGHT: _____
_____
_____
_____

YOUR PRAYER
REQUEST: _____
_____
_____
_____
_____
_____
_____
_____
_____

DATES PRAYERS
ANSWERED: _____
_____
_____
_____

DATE_____

DAY 102

For thou shalt be a witness unto all men of what thou hast seen and heard. *Acts 22:15*

Key Thought: Take God's message everywhere.

YOUR KEY
THOUGHT: _____
_____
_____
_____

YOUR PRAYER
REQUEST: _____
_____
_____
_____
_____
_____
_____
_____

DATES PRAYERS
ANSWERED: _____
_____
_____
_____

DAY 103

And now, Israel what doth the LORD thy God require of thee, but to fear the Lord thy God, to walk in all his ways, and to love him, and to serve the Lord thy God with all thy heart, and with all thy soul. *Deut. 10:12*

Key Thought: Fear God, do His will, worship Him completely.

YOUR KEY
THOUGHT: _____

_____

_____

_____

YOUR PRAYER
REQUEST: _____

_____

_____

_____

_____

_____

_____

_____

DATES PRAYERS
ANSWERED: _____

_____

_____

_____

DAY 104

But take diligent need to do the commandment and the law, which Moses the servant of the LORD charged you, to love the LORD your God, and to walk in all his ways, and to keep his commandments, and to cleave to him, and to serve him with all thy heart and with all your soul. *Josh.22:5*

Key Thought: Keep God's commandments.

YOUR KEY
THOUGHT: _____
_____
_____
_____

YOUR PRAYER
REQUEST: _____
_____
_____
_____
_____
_____
_____
_____

DATES PRAYERS
ANSWERED: _____
_____
_____
_____

DAY 105

He hath shewed thee, O man what is good; and what doth the LORD require of thee, but to do justly, and to love mercy, and to walk humbly with thy God. *Mic.6:8*

Key Thought: Walk humbly with God.

YOUR KEY
THOUGHT: _____
_____
_____
_____

YOUR PRAYER
REQUEST: _____
_____
_____
_____
_____
_____
_____
_____

DATES PRAYERS
ANSWERED: _____
_____
_____
_____

DAY 106

But the Comforter, which is the Holy Ghost, whom the Father will send in my name, he shall teach you all things; and bring all things to your remembrance, whatsoever I have said unto you. *John 14:26*

Key Thought: The Holy Spirit is our teacher.

YOUR KEY
THOUGHT: _____
_____
_____
_____

YOUR PRAYER
REQUEST: _____
_____
_____
_____
_____
_____
_____
_____

DATES PRAYERS
ANSWERED: _____
_____
_____
_____

DAY 107

If any of you lack wisdom, let him ask of God, That giveth to all men liberally, and unbraideth not and it shall be given. *James 1:5*

Key Thought: Pray for wisdom, it shall be given.

YOUR KEY
THOUGHT: _____
_____
_____
_____

YOUR PRAYER
REQUEST: _____
_____
_____
_____
_____
_____
_____
_____

DATES PRAYERS
ANSWERED: _____
_____
_____
_____

DAY 108

Trust in the LORD with all thine heart, and lean not unto thine own understanding. In all thy ways acknowledge him, and he shall direct thy path. *Prov.3:5,6*

Key Thought: Trust in the Lord, he will direct you.

YOUR KEY
THOUGHT: _____
_____
_____
_____

YOUR PRAYER
REQUEST: _____
_____
_____
_____
_____
_____
_____
_____

DATES PRAYERS
ANSWERED: _____
_____
_____
_____

DAY 109

Then we which are alive and remain shall be caught up together with them in the clouds, to meet the Lord in the air; and so shall we ever be with the Lord. Wherefore comfort one another with these words. *1 Thes. 4:17,18*

YOUR KEY
THOUGHT: _____

_____

_____

_____

YOUR PRAYER
REQUEST: _____

_____

_____

_____

_____

_____

_____

_____

DATES PRAYERS
ANSWERED: _____

_____

_____

_____

DAY 110

And ye shall be hated of all man for my name's sake; but he that endureth to the end shall be saved. *Matt. 10:22*

YOUR KEY
THOUGHT: _____
_____
_____
_____

YOUR PRAYER
REQUEST: _____
_____
_____
_____
_____
_____
_____
_____

DATES PRAYERS
ANSWERED: _____
_____
_____
_____

DAY 111

For I have satiated the weary soul, and I have replenished every sorrowful soul. *Jer. 31:25*

Key Thought: God gives rest to the weary.

YOUR KEY
THOUGHT: _____
_____
_____
_____

YOUR PRAYER
REQUEST: _____
_____
_____
_____
_____
_____
_____
_____

DATES PRAYERS
ANSWERED: _____
_____
_____
_____

DAY 112

And thine ears shall hear a word behind thee saying, this is the way, walk ye in it, when ye turn to the right hand, and when ye turn to the left.

Key Thought: Hear what God is saying to you.

YOUR KEY
THOUGHT: _____
_____
_____
_____

YOUR PRAYER
REQUEST: _____
_____
_____
_____
_____
_____
_____
_____

DATES PRAYERS
ANSWERED: _____
_____
_____
_____

DAY 113

Wash me thoroughly from iniquity and cleanse me from my sin. *Ps.51:2*

Key Thought: God will cleanse you from your sins.

YOUR KEY
THOUGHT: _____

_____

_____

_____

YOUR PRAYER
REQUEST: _____

_____

_____

_____

_____

_____

_____

_____

DATES PRAYERS
ANSWERED: _____

_____

_____

_____

DAY 114

But even the very hairs of your head are all numbered. Fear not therefore, ye are of more value than many sparrows. *Luke 12:7*

Key Thought: The hairs on your head are numbered.

YOUR KEY
THOUGHT: _____
_____
_____
_____

YOUR PRAYER
REQUEST: _____
_____
_____
_____
_____
_____
_____
_____

DATES PRAYERS
ANSWERED: _____
_____
_____
_____

DAY 115

I know that there is no good in them, but for a man to rejoice, and to do good in his life. *Eccl. 3:12*

Key Thought: Be happy and do good in life.

YOUR KEY
THOUGHT: _____

_____

_____

_____

YOUR PRAYER
REQUEST: _____

_____

_____

_____

_____

_____

_____

_____

DATES PRAYERS
ANSWERED: _____

_____

_____

_____

DAY 116

Blessed is the man that walketh not in the counsel of the ungodly, nor standeth in the way of sinners, nor sitteth in the seat of the scornful. *Ps. 1:1*

Key Thought: Avoid counsel of wicked.

YOUR KEY
THOUGHT: _____
_____
_____
_____

YOUR PRAYER
REQUEST: _____
_____
_____
_____
_____
_____
_____
_____
_____

DATES PRAYERS
ANSWERED: _____
_____
_____
_____

DAY 117

I will bless the LORD at all times; his praise shall continually be in my mouth. *Ps.34:1*

Key Thought: I will praise the Lord at all times.

YOUR KEY
THOUGHT: _____
_____
_____
_____

YOUR PRAYER
REQUEST: _____
_____
_____
_____
_____
_____
_____
_____

DATES PRAYERS
ANSWERED: _____
_____
_____
_____

DAY 118

HARDEN NOT YOUR HEARTS, AS IN THE PROVOCATION, IN THE DAY OF TEMPTATION IN THE WILDERNESS. *HEB.3:8*

Key Thought: Do not harden your hearts.

YOUR KEY
THOUGHT: _____
_____
_____
_____

YOUR PRAYER
REQUEST: _____
_____
_____
_____
_____
_____
_____
_____

DATES PRAYERS
ANSWERED: _____
_____
_____
_____

DAY 119

Create in me a clean heart, O God; and renew a right spirit within me. *Ps.51:10*

Key Thought: God can create a clean heart.

YOUR KEY
THOUGHT: _____
_____
_____
_____

YOUR PRAYER
REQUEST: _____
_____
_____
_____
_____
_____
_____
_____

DATES PRAYERS
ANSWERED: _____
_____
_____
_____

DAY 120

Casting all your care upon him; for he careth for you. *1Pet.5:7*

Key Thought: Give all your cares to God.

YOUR KEY
THOUGHT: _____
_____
_____
_____

YOUR PRAYER
REQUEST: _____
_____
_____
_____
_____
_____
_____
_____
_____

DATES PRAYERS
ANSWERED: _____
_____
_____
_____

DATE_____

DAY 121

What? know ye not that your body is the temple of the Holy Ghost which is in you, which ye have of God and ye are not your own? *1Cor. 6:19*

Key Thought: Your body is the temple of the Holy Ghost.

YOUR KEY
THOUGHT: _____
_____
_____
_____

YOUR PRAYER
REQUEST: _____
_____
_____
_____
_____
_____
_____
_____

DATES PRAYERS
ANSWERED: _____
_____
_____
_____

DAY 122
Quench not the Spirit. *1Thess.5:19*

Key Thought: Do not quench the Holy Spirit.

YOUR KEY
THOUGHT: _____
_____
_____
_____

YOUR PRAYER
REQUEST: _____
_____
_____
_____
_____
_____
_____
_____

DATES PRAYERS
ANSWERED: _____
_____
_____
_____

DAY 123

There is no fear in love; but perfect love casteth out fear; because fear hath torment. He that feareth is not made perfect in love. *1John 4:18*

Key Thought: Fear has torment.

YOUR KEY
THOUGHT: _____
_____
_____
_____

YOUR PRAYER
REQUEST: _____
_____
_____
_____
_____
_____
_____
_____

DATES PRAYERS
ANSWERED: _____
_____
_____
_____

DAY 124

Hereby know we that we dwell in him, and he in us, because he hath given us his spirit. *1John 4:13*

Key Thought: God has given us His spirit.

YOUR KEY
THOUGHT: _____
_____
_____
_____

YOUR PRAYER
REQUEST: _____
_____
_____
_____
_____
_____
_____
_____

DATES PRAYERS
ANSWERED: _____
_____
_____
_____

DAY 125

And have hope towards God, which they themselves also allow that there shall be resurrection of the dead, both of the just and the unjust. *Acts 24:15*

Key Thought: Just and the unjust that are dead shall be resurrected from the dead.

YOUR KEY
THOUGHT: _____
_____
_____
_____

YOUR PRAYER
REQUEST: _____
_____
_____
_____
_____
_____
_____
_____

DATES PRAYERS
ANSWERED: _____
_____
_____
_____

DATE_____

DAY 126
The meek also shall increase their joy in the LORD, and the poor among men shall rejoice in the Holy One of Israel. *Is. 29:19*

Key Thought: The meek and the poor shall rejoice.

YOUR KEY
THOUGHT: _____
_____
_____
_____

YOUR PRAYER
REQUEST: _____
_____
_____
_____
_____
_____
_____
_____

DATES PRAYERS
ANSWERED: _____
_____
_____
_____

DAY 127

Bless them that persecute you; bless, and curse not. *Rom. 12:14*

Key Thought: Feed your hungry enemies.

YOUR KEY
THOUGHT: _____
_____
_____
_____

YOUR PRAYER
REQUEST: _____
_____
_____
_____
_____
_____
_____
_____

DATES PRAYERS
ANSWERED: _____
_____
_____
_____

DAY 128

And why call ye me Lord, Lord, and do not the things which I say? *Luke 6:46*

Key Thought: Hypocrites call on the Lord, but do not obey him.

YOUR KEY
THOUGHT: _____
_____
_____
_____

YOUR PRAYER
REQUEST: _____
_____
_____
_____
_____
_____
_____
_____
_____

DATES PRAYERS
ANSWERED: _____
_____
_____
_____

DAY 129

And God said unto Moses, I AM THAT I AM; and he said, Thus shalt thou say unto the children of Israel I AM hath sent me unto you. *Ex. 3:14*

Key Thought: I AM THAT I AM

YOUR KEY
THOUGHT: _____

_____

_____

_____

YOUR PRAYER
REQUEST: _____

_____

_____

_____

_____

_____

_____

_____

DATES PRAYERS
ANSWERED: _____

_____

_____

_____

DAY 130

O that ye would altogether hold your peace and it should be wisdom. *Job 13:5*

Key Thought: Think before speaking.

YOUR KEY
THOUGHT: _____

_____

_____

_____

YOUR PRAYER
REQUEST: _____

_____

_____

_____

_____

_____

_____

_____

DATES PRAYERS
ANSWERED: _____

_____

_____

_____

DATE_____

DAY 131

For even when we were with you, this we commanded you, that if any would not work, neither should he eat. *2Thess. 3:10*

Key Thought: Work not, eat not.

YOUR KEY
THOUGHT: _____
_____
_____
_____

YOUR PRAYER
REQUEST: _____
_____
_____
_____
_____
_____
_____
_____

DATES PRAYERS
ANSWERED: _____
_____
_____
_____

DAY 132

Know ye not that the unrighteous shall not inherit the kingdom of God? Be not deceived neither fornicator, nor idolaters, nor adulterers, nor effeminate, nor abusers of themselves with mankind. *1Cor.6:9*

Key Thought: The unrighteous shall not inherit the kingdom of God.

YOUR KEY
THOUGHT: _____
_____
_____
_____

YOUR PRAYER
REQUEST: _____
_____
_____
_____
_____
_____
_____
_____

DATES PRAYERS
ANSWERED: _____
_____
_____
_____

DAY 133

Also that the soul be without knowledge, it is not good; and he that hasteth with his feet sinneth. *Prov. 19:2*

Key Thought: Zeal without knowledge is not good.

YOUR KEY
THOUGHT: _____
_____
_____
_____

YOUR PRAYER
REQUEST: _____
_____
_____
_____
_____
_____
_____
_____

DATES PRAYERS
ANSWERED: _____
_____
_____
_____

DAY 134

Let no man deceive himself. if any man among you seemeth to be wise in this world, let him become a fool, that he may be wise.

YOUR KEY
THOUGHT: _____
_____
_____
_____

YOUR PRAYER
REQUEST: _____
_____
_____
_____
_____
_____
_____
_____

DATES PRAYERS
ANSWERED: _____
_____
_____
_____

DAY 135

He that saith he abideth in him ought himself also so to walk, even as he walked. *1John 2:6*

Key Thought: Walk as Jesus walked.

YOUR KEY
THOUGHT: _____
_____
_____
_____

YOUR PRAYER
REQUEST: _____
_____
_____
_____
_____
_____
_____
_____

DATES PRAYERS
ANSWERED: _____
_____
_____
_____

DAY 136

And ye become followers of us and of the Lord, having received the word in much affliction, with joy of the Holy Ghost. *1Thess. 1:6*

Key Thought: Receive the word in affliction with joy of the Holy Ghost.

YOUR KEY
THOUGHT: _____
_____
_____
_____

YOUR PRAYER
REQUEST: _____
_____
_____
_____
_____
_____
_____
_____

DATES PRAYERS
ANSWERED: _____
_____
_____
_____

DAY 137

Having your conversation honest among the Gentiles that whereas they speak against you as evildoers they may by your good works, which they shall behold glorify God in the day of visitation. *1 Pet.2:12*

Key Thought: Let your good works speak for you.

YOUR KEY
THOUGHT: _____
_____
_____
_____

YOUR PRAYER
REQUEST: _____
_____
_____
_____
_____
_____
_____
_____

DATES PRAYERS
ANSWERED: _____
_____
_____
_____

DAY 138

And he said unto them, Is a candle brought to be put under a bushel, or under a bed? And not to be set on a candlestick? *Mark 4:21*

Key Thought: Let your light shine.

YOUR KEY
THOUGHT: _____
_____
_____
_____

YOUR PRAYER
REQUEST: _____
_____
_____
_____
_____
_____
_____
_____
_____

DATES PRAYERS
ANSWERED: _____
_____
_____
_____

DAY 139

But let him ask in faith, nothing wavering. For he that wavereth is like a wave of the sea driven with the wind and tossed. *James 1:6*

Key Thought: Doubtful minds are unsettled.

YOUR KEY
THOUGHT: _____
_____
_____
_____

YOUR PRAYER
REQUEST: _____
_____
_____
_____
_____
_____
_____
_____

DATES PRAYERS
ANSWERED: _____
_____
_____
_____

DAY 140

No man can serve two masters; for either he will hate one, and love the other; or else he will hold to one, and despise the other. Ye cannot serve God and mammon. *Matt. 6:24*

Key Thought: No man can serve the Lord and the devil.

YOUR KEY
THOUGHT: _____

_____

_____

_____

YOUR PRAYER
REQUEST: _____

_____

_____

_____

_____

_____

_____

_____

DATES PRAYERS
ANSWERED: _____

_____

_____

_____

DAY 141

And, ye fathers, provoke not your children to wrath; but bring them up in the nurture and admonition of the Lord. Eph.6:4

Key Thought: Bring your children up in the things of the Lord.

YOUR KEY
THOUGHT: _____
_____
_____
_____

YOUR PRAYER
REQUEST: _____
_____
_____
_____
_____
_____
_____
_____

DATES PRAYERS
ANSWERED: _____
_____
_____
_____

DAY 142

Finally, brethren, whatsoever things are true, whatsoever things are honest, whatsoever things are just, whatsoever things are pure, whatsoever things are lovely, whatsoever things are of good report; if there be any virtue, and if there be any praise, think on these things. *Phil. 4:8*

Key Thought: Fix your mind on what is true, honorable, and just.

YOUR KEY
THOUGHT: _____
_____
_____
_____

YOUR PRAYER
REQUEST: _____
_____
_____
_____
_____
_____
_____
_____

DATES PRAYERS
ANSWERED: _____
_____
_____
_____

DAY 143

Be careful for nothing; but in everything by prayer and supplication with thanksgiving let your request be made known unto God. *Phil. 4:6*

Key Thought: Be anxious for nothing.

YOUR KEY
THOUGHT: _____
_____
_____
_____

YOUR PRAYER
REQUEST: _____
_____
_____
_____
_____
_____
_____
_____

DATES PRAYERS
ANSWERED: _____
_____
_____
_____

DAY 144

The just man walketh in his integrity, his children are blessed after him. *Prov. 20:7*

Key Thought: The just man walks in his integrity.

YOUR KEY
THOUGHT: _____
_____
_____
_____

YOUR PRAYER
REQUEST: _____
_____
_____
_____
_____
_____
_____
_____

DATES PRAYERS
ANSWERED: _____
_____
_____
_____

DAY 145

For God hath not called us unto uncleanness, but unto holiness. *1 Thess 4:7*

Key Thought: Be clean, be holy.

YOUR KEY
THOUGHT: _____
_____
_____
_____

YOUR PRAYER
REQUEST: _____
_____
_____
_____
_____
_____
_____
_____

DATES PRAYERS
ANSWERED: _____
_____
_____
_____

DAY 146

Is any man sick among you? Let him call for the elders of the church; and let them pray over him, anointing him with oil in the name of the Lord. *James 5:14*

Key Thought: Let the elders pray over the sick.

YOUR KEY
THOUGHT: _____
_____
_____
_____

YOUR PRAYER
REQUEST: _____
_____
_____
_____
_____
_____
_____
_____

DATES PRAYERS
ANSWERED: _____
_____
_____
_____

DAY 147

And it came to pass, as Jesus sat at meat in the house, behold many publicans and sinners came and sat down with him and his disciple. *Matt. 9:10*

Key Thought: All types of people will sit among you.

YOUR KEY
THOUGHT: _____
_____
_____
_____

YOUR PRAYER
REQUEST: _____
_____
_____
_____
_____
_____
_____
_____

DATES PRAYERS
ANSWERED: _____
_____
_____
_____

DAY 148

And he commanded us to preach unto the people, and to testify that it is he which was ordained of God to be the Judge of quick and dead. *Acts 10:42*

Key Thought: Jesus to judge the living and the dead.

YOUR KEY
THOUGHT: _____
_____
_____
_____

YOUR PRAYER
REQUEST: _____
_____
_____
_____
_____
_____
_____
_____
_____

DATES PRAYERS
ANSWERED: _____
_____
_____
_____

DAY 149

Finally, be ye all of one mind, having compassion one of another, love as brethren, be pitiful, be courteous. *1Pet. 3:8*

Key Thought: Be compassionate and humble.

YOUR KEY
THOUGHT: _____
_____
_____
_____

YOUR PRAYER
REQUEST: _____
_____
_____
_____
_____
_____
_____
_____

DATES PRAYERS
ANSWERED: _____
_____
_____
_____

DAY 150

And the Lord said unto him, Now do ye Pharisees make clean the outside of the cup and the platter; but your inward part is full of ravening and wickedness. *Lk. 11:39*

Key Thought: Hypocrites are clean on the outside, yet filthy on the inside.

YOUR KEY
THOUGHT: _____
_____
_____
_____

YOUR PRAYER
REQUEST: _____
_____
_____
_____
_____
_____
_____
_____

DATES PRAYERS
ANSWERED: _____
_____
_____
_____

DAY 151

He that committeth sin is of the devil; for the devil sinneth from the beginning. For this purpose the Son of God was manifested, that he might destroy the works of devil. *1Jn. 3:8*

Key Thought: The Son of God came to destroy the works of the devil.

YOUR KEY
THOUGHT: _____
_____
_____
_____

YOUR PRAYER
REQUEST: _____
_____
_____
_____
_____
_____
_____
_____

DATES PRAYERS
ANSWERED: _____
_____
_____
_____

DAY 152

For even hereunto were ye called; because Christ also suffered for us leaving us an example, that ye should follow his steps. *1Pet. 2:21*

Key Thought: Jesus left examples for us to follow.

YOUR KEY
THOUGHT: _____
_____
_____
_____

YOUR PRAYER
REQUEST: _____
_____
_____
_____
_____
_____
_____
_____

DATES PRAYERS
ANSWERED: _____
_____
_____
_____

DAY 153

Watch and pray, that ye enter not into temptation; the spirit indeed is willing, but the flesh is weak. *Matt. 26:41*

Key Thought: Be aware of temptation.

YOUR KEY
THOUGHT: _____

_____

_____

_____

YOUR PRAYER
REQUEST: _____

_____

_____

_____

_____

_____

_____

_____

DATES PRAYERS
ANSWERED: _____

_____

_____

_____

DAY 154

The wicked desireth the net of evil men; but the root of righteous yieldeth fruit. *Prov. 12:12*

Key Thought: The righteous will yield fruit.

YOUR KEY
THOUGHT: _____
_____
_____
_____

YOUR PRAYER
REQUEST: _____
_____
_____
_____
_____
_____
_____
_____

DATES PRAYERS
ANSWERED: _____
_____
_____
_____

DAY 155

Whatsoever thy hand findeth to do, do it with thy might; for there is no work, not device, nor knowledge, nor wisdom, in the grave whither thou goest. *Eccles. 9:10*

Key Thought: Whatever you do, do it well.

YOUR KEY
THOUGHT: _____
_____
_____
_____

YOUR PRAYER
REQUEST: _____
_____
_____
_____
_____
_____
_____
_____

DATES PRAYERS
ANSWERED: _____
_____
_____
_____

DAY 156

And the angel answered and said unto her, THE HOLY GHOST shall come upon thee, and the power of the Highest shall overshadow thee; therefore also that holy thing which shall be born of thee shall be called the Son of God. *Lk. 1:35*

Key Thought: Jesus born holy.

YOUR KEY
THOUGHT: _____
_____
_____
_____

YOUR PRAYER
REQUEST: _____
_____
_____
_____
_____
_____
_____
_____

DATES PRAYERS
ANSWERED: _____
_____
_____
_____

DAY 157

And he said, The LORD is my rock, and my fortress, and my deliverer; *2Sam. 22:2*

Key Thought: The Lord is my deliverer.

YOUR KEY
THOUGHT: _____
_____
_____
_____

YOUR PRAYER
REQUEST: _____
_____
_____
_____
_____
_____
_____
_____

DATES PRAYERS
ANSWERED: _____
_____
_____
_____

DAY 158

Jesus saith unto him, Thomas, because thou hast seen me, thou hast believed; blessed are they that have not seen, and yet have believed. *Jn. 20:29*

Key Thought: Faith sees what your eyes cannot.

YOUR KEY
THOUGHT: _____
_____
_____
_____

YOUR PRAYER
REQUEST: _____
_____
_____
_____
_____
_____
_____
_____

DATES PRAYERS
ANSWERED: _____
_____
_____
_____

DAY 159

I waited patiently for the LORD; and he inclined unto me. and heard my cry. *Ps. 40:1*

Key Thought: Wait patiently on the Lord.

YOUR KEY
THOUGHT: _____

_____

_____

_____

YOUR PRAYER
REQUEST: _____

_____

_____

_____

_____

_____

_____

_____

_____

DATES PRAYERS
ANSWERED: _____

_____

_____

_____

DAY 160
And he said unto me, My grace is sufficient for thee: for my strength is made perfect in weakness. Most gladly therefore will I rather glory in my infirmities, that the power of Christ may rest upon me. *2Cor.12:9*

Key Thought: Gods grace is sufficient.

YOUR KEY
THOUGHT: _____
_____
_____
_____

YOUR PRAYER
REQUEST: _____
_____
_____
_____
_____
_____
_____

DATES PRAYERS
ANSWERED: _____
_____
_____
_____

DAY 161

And go quickly, and tell his disciples that he is risen from the dead; and behold, he goeth before you into Gal'lee; there shall ye see him; lo I have told you. *Matt. 28:7*

Key Thought: Do not hasten to deliver Gods word.

YOUR KEY
THOUGHT: _____
_____
_____
_____

YOUR PRAYER
REQUEST: _____
_____
_____
_____
_____
_____
_____
_____

DATES PRAYERS
ANSWERED: _____
_____
_____
_____

DAY 162

The foolish shall not stand in thy sight; thou hatest all workers of iniquity. *Ps.5:5*

Key Thought: Hate all who do evil.

YOUR KEY
THOUGHT: _____
_____
_____
_____

YOUR PRAYER
REQUEST: _____
_____
_____
_____
_____
_____
_____
_____

DATES PRAYERS
ANSWERED: _____
_____
_____
_____

DAY 163

But chiefly them that walk after the flesh in the lust of uncleanness, and despise government. Presumptuous *are they*, selfwilled, they are not afraid to speak evil of dignities. *2Pet 2:10*

Key Thought: Avoid lustful desires.

YOUR KEY
THOUGHT: _____
_____
_____
_____

YOUR PRAYER
REQUEST: _____
_____
_____
_____
_____
_____
_____
_____

DATES PRAYERS
ANSWERED: _____
_____
_____
_____

DAY 164

If ye then be risen with Christ, seek those things which are above where Christ sitteth on the right hand of God. Set your affection on things above, not on things on the earth. *Col. 3:1,2*

Key Thought: Let your thoughts be filled from heaven.

YOUR KEY
THOUGHT: _____
_____
_____
_____

YOUR PRAYER
REQUEST: _____
_____
_____
_____
_____
_____
_____
_____

DATES PRAYERS
ANSWERED: _____
_____
_____
_____

DAY 165

For I know their works and their thoughts it shall come, that I will gather all nations and tongues; and they shall come see my glory. *Is. 66:18*

Key Thought: Gods know your plan and your heart.

YOUR KEY
THOUGHT: _____
_____
_____
_____

YOUR PRAYER
REQUEST: _____
_____
_____
_____
_____
_____
_____
_____

DATES PRAYERS
ANSWERED: _____
_____
_____
_____

DAY 166

And God, which knoweth the hearts, bare them witness, giving them the Holy Ghost, even as he did unto us. *Acts 15:8*

Key Thought: God knows the heart.

YOUR KEY
THOUGHT: _____
_____
_____
_____

YOUR PRAYER
REQUEST: _____
_____
_____
_____
_____
_____
_____
_____

DATES PRAYERS
ANSWERED: _____
_____
_____
_____

DAY 167

O LORD, thou hast searched me, and know me. *Ps. 139:1*

Key Thought: God knows everything about us.

YOUR KEY
THOUGHT: _____
_____
_____
_____

YOUR PRAYER
REQUEST: _____
_____
_____
_____
_____
_____
_____
_____

DATES PRAYERS
ANSWERED: _____
_____
_____
_____

DAY 168

He that hath a froward heart findeth no good: and he that hath a perverse tongue falleth into mischief. *Prov. 17:20*

Key Thought: A crooked heart will not proper.

YOUR KEY
THOUGHT: _____
_____
_____
_____

YOUR PRAYER
REQUEST: _____
_____
_____
_____
_____
_____
_____
_____

DATES PRAYERS
ANSWERED: _____
_____
_____
_____

DAY 169

HEAVEN IS MY THRONE, AND EARTH IS MY FOOTSTOOL: WHATHOUSE YE BUILD ME? SAITH THE LORD OR WHAT IS THE PLACE OF MY REST? *Acts 7:49*

Key Thought: Heaven is my throne.

YOUR KEY
THOUGHT: _____
_____
_____
_____

YOUR PRAYER
REQUEST: _____
_____
_____
_____
_____
_____
_____
_____

DATES PRAYERS
ANSWERED: _____
_____
_____
_____

DAY 170

Let us therefore come boldly unto the throne of grace, that we may obtain mercy, and find grace to help in time of need. *Heb. 4:16*

Key Thought: Go boldly unto the throne of grace.

YOUR KEY
THOUGHT: _____
_____
_____
_____

YOUR PRAYER
REQUEST: _____
_____
_____
_____
_____
_____
_____
_____

DATES PRAYERS
ANSWERED: _____
_____
_____
_____

DAY 171

And in hell he lift up his eyes, being in torments, and seeth Abraham afar off, and Lar'-a-rus in his bosom. *Lk. 16:23*

Key Thought: Hell is a place torment.

YOUR KEY
THOUGHT: _____
_____
_____
_____

YOUR PRAYER
REQUEST: _____
_____
_____
_____
_____
_____
_____
_____

DATES PRAYERS
ANSWERED: _____
_____
_____
_____

DAY 172

The angels of the LORD encampeth round about them that fear him, and delivereth them. *Ps.34:7*

Key Thought: God has help for those that fear him.

YOUR KEY
THOUGHT: _____
_____
_____
_____

YOUR PRAYER
REQUEST: _____
_____
_____
_____
_____
_____
_____
_____

DATES PRAYERS
ANSWERED: _____
_____
_____
_____

DAY 173

Casting all your care upon him; for he careth for you. *1Pet.5:7*

Key Thought: Cast cares unto God.

YOUR KEY
THOUGHT: _____

_____

_____

_____

YOUR PRAYER
REQUEST: _____

_____

_____

_____

_____

_____

_____

_____

DATES PRAYERS
ANSWERED: _____

_____

_____

_____

DAY 174

Let your conversation be without covetousness; and be content with such things as ye have; for he hath said I WILL NEVER LEAVE THEE, NOR FORSAKE THEE. *Heb.13:5*

Key Thought: God will never leave you nor forsake you.

YOUR KEY
THOUGHT: _____
_____
_____
_____

YOUR PRAYER
REQUEST: _____
_____
_____
_____
_____
_____
_____
_____

DATES PRAYERS
ANSWERED: _____
_____
_____
_____

DAY 175

If ye then, being evil, know how to give good gifts unto your children: how much more shall your heavenly Father give the Holy Spirit to them that ask him? *Lk. 11:13*

Key Thought: Ask and the Holy Spirit is fully given.

YOUR KEY
THOUGHT: _____
_____
_____
_____

YOUR PRAYER
REQUEST: _____
_____
_____
_____
_____
_____
_____
_____

DATES PRAYERS
ANSWERED: _____
_____
_____
_____

DAY 176

For the kingdom of God is not meat and drink; but righteousness and peace, and joy in the Holy Ghost. *Rom. 14:17*

Key Thought: There is joy in the Holy Ghost.

YOUR KEY
THOUGHT: _____
_____
_____
_____

YOUR PRAYER
REQUEST: _____
_____
_____
_____
_____
_____
_____
_____

DATES PRAYERS
ANSWERED: _____
_____
_____
_____

DAY 177

For by one Spirit are we all baptized into one body, whether us be Jews or Gentiles, whether *we* be bond or free; and have been all made to drink into one Spirit. *1Cor. 12:13*

Key Thought: Believers are all baptized in one Spirit. (Holy Spirit)

YOUR KEY
THOUGHT: _____

_____

_____

_____

YOUR PRAYER
REQUEST: _____

_____

_____

_____

_____

_____

_____

_____

DATES PRAYERS
ANSWERED: _____

_____

_____

_____

DAY 178

Blessed are the pure in heart for they shall see God. *Matt. 5:8*

Key Thought: God blesses those that has a pure heart.

YOUR KEY
THOUGHT: _____

_____

_____

_____

YOUR PRAYER
REQUEST: _____

_____

_____

_____

_____

_____

_____

_____

DATES PRAYERS
ANSWERED: _____

_____

_____

_____

DAY 179

Lay hands suddenly on no man, neither be partakers of other men's sin: keep thyself pure.
1Tim. 5:22

Key Thought: Keep yourself pure.

YOUR KEY
THOUGHT: _____

_____

_____

_____

YOUR PRAYER
REQUEST: _____

_____

_____

_____

_____

_____

_____

DATES PRAYERS
ANSWERED: _____

_____

_____

_____

DAY 180

What? Know ye not that your body is the temple of the Holy Ghost which is in you, which ye have of God and ye are not your own? *1Cor. 6:19*

Key Thought: Your body is the temple of t he Holy Ghost.

YOUR KEY
THOUGHT: _____
_____
_____
_____

YOUR PRAYER
REQUEST: _____
_____
_____
_____
_____
_____
_____
_____

DATES PRAYERS
ANSWERED: _____
_____
_____
_____

DAY 181

Go ye therefore, and teach all nations, baptizing them in the name of the Father, and of the Son, and of the Holy Ghost: *Matt 28:19*

Key Thought: Tell everyone about the divine Trinity.

YOUR KEY
THOUGHT: _____
_____
_____
_____

YOUR PRAYER
REQUEST: _____
_____
_____
_____
_____
_____
_____
_____

DATES PRAYERS
ANSWERED: _____
_____
_____
_____

DAY 182

Providing for honest things, not only in the sight of the Lord, but also in the sight of men.
2 Cor. 8:21

Key Thought: Be honest at all times.

YOUR KEY
THOUGHT: _____
_____
_____
_____

YOUR PRAYER
REQUEST: _____
_____
_____
_____
_____
_____
_____
_____
_____

DATES PRAYERS
ANSWERED: _____
_____
_____
_____

DAY 183

He that speaketh truth sheweth forth righteousness; but a false witness deceit.
Prov. 12:17

Key Thought: Truthful witness gives an honest testimony.

YOUR KEY
THOUGHT: _____

_____

_____

_____

YOUR PRAYER
REQUEST: _____

_____

_____

_____

_____

_____

_____

_____

DATES PRAYERS
ANSWERED: _____

_____

_____

_____

DAY 184

I will praise the name of God will a song, and will magnify him with thanksgiving. *Ps. 69:30*

Key Thought: Honor God with praise and thanksgiving.

YOUR KEY
THOUGHT: _____
_____
_____
_____

YOUR PRAYER
REQUEST: _____
_____
_____
_____
_____
_____
_____
_____

DATES PRAYERS
ANSWERED: _____
_____
_____
_____

DAY 185

Be of good courage, and he shall strengthen your heart, all ye that hope in the LORD. *Ps. 31:24*

Key Thought: Be strong in the Lord.

YOUR KEY
THOUGHT: _____

_____

_____

_____

YOUR PRAYER
REQUEST: _____

_____

_____

_____

_____

_____

_____

_____

DATES PRAYERS
ANSWERED: _____

_____

_____

_____

DAY 186

Be not forgetful to entertain strangers; for thereby some have entertained angels unawares. *Heb. 13:2*

Key Thought: Strangers may be angels.

YOUR KEY
THOUGHT: _____
_____
_____
_____

YOUR PRAYER
REQUEST: _____
_____
_____
_____
_____
_____
_____
_____

DATES PRAYERS
ANSWERED: _____
_____
_____
_____

DAY 187

Let all bitterness and wrath, and anger, and clamour, and evil speaking, be put away from you, with all malice: And be ye kind one to another tender hearted, forgiving one another, even as God for Christ's sake hath forgiven you. *Eph. 4:31,32*

Key Thought: Forgive others as God has forgiven you.

YOUR KEY
THOUGHT: _____
_____
_____
_____

YOUR PRAYER
REQUEST: _____
_____
_____
_____
_____
_____
_____
_____

DATES PRAYERS
ANSWERED: _____
_____
_____
_____

DAY 188

For I am persuaded, that neither death nor life, nor angels, nor principalities, nor powers, nor things present, nor things to come, nor height, nor depth, nor any other creature, shall be able to separate us from the love of God, which is in Christ Jesus our Lord. *Rom. 8:38,39*

Key Thought: Nothing can separate me from the love of God.

YOUR KEY
THOUGHT: _____
_____
_____
_____

YOUR PRAYER
REQUEST: _____
_____
_____
_____
_____
_____
_____
_____

DATES PRAYERS
ANSWERED: _____
_____
_____
_____

DAY 189

He will swallow up death in victory and the LORD God will wipe away tears from off all faces. *Is. 25:8*

Key Thought: In death there is victory.

YOUR KEY
THOUGHT: _____

_____

_____

_____

YOUR PRAYER
REQUEST: _____

_____

_____

_____

_____

_____

_____

_____

DATES PRAYERS
ANSWERED: _____

_____

_____

_____

DAY 190

The LORD also will be a refuge from the oppressed, a refuge in times of trouble. *Ps. 9:9*

Key Thought: The Lord is our refuge.

YOUR KEY
THOUGHT: _____
_____
_____
_____

YOUR PRAYER
REQUEST: _____
_____
_____
_____
_____
_____
_____
_____

DATES PRAYERS
ANSWERED: _____
_____
_____
_____

DAY 191

I will praise the LORD according to his righteousness: and will sing praise to the name of the LORD most high. *Ps. 7:17*

Key Thought: I will praise the Lord.

YOUR KEY
THOUGHT: _____
_____
_____
_____

YOUR PRAYER
REQUEST: _____
_____
_____
_____
_____
_____
_____
_____

DATES PRAYERS
ANSWERED: _____
_____
_____
_____

DAY 192

Thou hast put gladness in my heart, more than in the time that their corn and their wine increased. *Ps. 4:7*

Key Thought: God has given me an abundance of joy.

YOUR KEY
THOUGHT: _____
_____
_____
_____

YOUR PRAYER
REQUEST: _____
_____
_____
_____
_____
_____
_____
_____

DATES PRAYERS
ANSWERED: _____
_____
_____
_____

DAY 193

Every man according as he purposeth in his heart, so let him give; not grudgingly, or of necessity; for God loveth a cheerful giver. *2Cor. 9:7*

Key Thought: God loves a cheerful giver.

YOUR KEY
THOUGHT: _____
_____
_____
_____

YOUR PRAYER
REQUEST: _____
_____
_____
_____
_____
_____
_____
_____
_____

DATES PRAYERS
ANSWERED: _____
_____
_____
_____

DAY 194

He that despiseth his neighbor sinneth; but he that hath mercy on the poor, happy is he.
Prov. 14:21

Key Thought: To envy is a sin

YOUR KEY
THOUGHT: _____
_____
_____
_____

YOUR PRAYER
REQUEST: _____
_____
_____
_____
_____
_____
_____
_____

DATES PRAYERS
ANSWERED: _____
_____
_____
_____

DAY 195

But as touching brotherly love ye need not that I write unto you; for ye yourself are taught of God to love one another. *1Thess. 4:9*

Key Thought: God teaches us to love one another

YOUR KEY
THOUGHT: _____
_____
_____
_____

YOUR PRAYER
REQUEST: _____
_____
_____
_____
_____
_____
_____
_____

DATES PRAYERS
ANSWERED: _____
_____
_____
_____

DATE_____

DAY 196
For we are labourers together with God: ye are God's husbandry, ye are God's building. *1Cor. 3:9*

Key Thought: We are labourers with God.

YOUR KEY
THOUGHT: _____
_____
_____
_____

YOUR PRAYER
REQUEST: _____
_____
_____
_____
_____
_____
_____
_____

DATES PRAYERS
ANSWERED: _____
_____
_____
_____

DAY 197

He that loveth his brother abideth in the light, and there is none occasion of stumbling in him. *1Jn. 2:12*

Key Thought: Loving our brother Jesus we shall have reason to stumble.

YOUR KEY
THOUGHT: _____
_____
_____
_____

YOUR PRAYER
REQUEST: _____
_____
_____
_____
_____
_____
_____
_____

DATES PRAYERS
ANSWERED: _____
_____
_____
_____

DAY 198

But godliness with contentment is great gain. For we brought nothing into this world, and it is certain we can carry nothing out. And having food and raiment let us be there with content. *1Tim. 6:6 - 8*

Key Thought: We brought nothing into this world and we shalt take nothing out.

YOUR KEY
THOUGHT: _____
_____
_____
_____

YOUR PRAYER
REQUEST: _____
_____
_____
_____
_____
_____
_____
_____

DATES PRAYERS
ANSWERED: _____
_____
_____
_____

DAY 199

A merry heart doeth good like a medicine; but a broken spirit drieth the bones. *Prov. 17:22*

Key Thought: A broken spirit will hinder you.

YOUR KEY
THOUGHT: _____
_____
_____
_____

YOUR PRAYER
REQUEST: _____
_____
_____
_____
_____
_____
_____
_____

DATES PRAYERS
ANSWERED: _____
_____
_____
_____

DAY 200

Fret not thyself because of evildoers, neither be thou envious against the workers of iniquity. For they shall soon be cut down like the grass, and wither as the green herb. *Ps. 37:1.2*

Key Thought: FRET NOT

YOUR KEY
THOUGHT: _____
_____
_____
_____

YOUR PRAYER
REQUEST: _____
_____
_____
_____
_____
_____
_____
_____

DATES PRAYERS
ANSWERED: _____
_____
_____
_____

DAY 201

If ye endure chastening, God dealeth with you as with sons; for what son is he whom the father chasteneth not? *Heb. 12:7*

Key Thought: God chastens his children.

YOUR KEY
THOUGHT: _____
_____
_____
_____

YOUR PRAYER
REQUEST: _____
_____
_____
_____
_____
_____
_____
_____

DATES PRAYERS
ANSWERED: _____
_____
_____
_____

DAY 202

For whom the LORD loveth he correcteth; even as a father the son in him he delighteth. *Prov. 3:12*

Key Thought: The Father corrects and yet is delighted in you.

YOUR KEY
THOUGHT: _____
_____
_____
_____

YOUR PRAYER
REQUEST: _____
_____
_____
_____
_____
_____
_____
_____

DATES PRAYERS
ANSWERED: _____
_____
_____
_____

DAY 203

He giveth power to the faint; and to *them that have* no might he increased strength. *Is. 40:29*

Key Thought: God will increase your strength.

YOUR KEY
THOUGHT: _____

_____

_____

_____

YOUR PRAYER
REQUEST: _____

_____

_____

_____

_____

_____

_____

DATES PRAYERS
ANSWERED: _____

_____

_____

_____

DAY 204

Wait on the LORD; be of good courage, and he shall strengthen thine heart: wait, I say on the LORD. *Ps. 27:4*

Key Thought: Wait on the Lord.

YOUR KEY
THOUGHT: _____
_____
_____
_____

YOUR PRAYER
REQUEST: _____
_____
_____
_____
_____
_____
_____
_____
_____

DATES PRAYERS
ANSWERED: _____
_____
_____
_____

DAY 205

Be strong and of good courage fear not, nor be afraid of them; for the LORD thy God he *it is* that doeth go with thee; he will not fail thee, nor forsake thee. *Deut. 31:6*

Key Thought: Fear not.

YOUR KEY
THOUGHT: _____
_____
_____
_____

YOUR PRAYER
REQUEST: _____
_____
_____
_____
_____
_____
_____
_____

DATES PRAYERS
ANSWERED: _____
_____
_____
_____

DAY 206

Fear the LORD your God is he that goeth with you, to fight for you against your enemies, to save you. *Deut. 20:4*

Key Thought: The battle is not yours, it's the Lord.

YOUR KEY
THOUGHT: _____
_____
_____
_____

YOUR PRAYER
REQUEST: _____
_____
_____
_____
_____
_____
_____
_____

DATES PRAYERS
ANSWERED: _____
_____
_____
_____

DAY 207

When a man's way please the LORD, he maketh even his enemies to be at peace with him.
Prov. 16:7

Key Thought: The Lord will cause your enemies to have peace with you.

YOUR KEY
THOUGHT: _____
_____
_____
_____

YOUR PRAYER
REQUEST: _____
_____
_____
_____
_____
_____
_____
_____

DATES PRAYERS
ANSWERED: _____
_____
_____
_____

DAY 208

And Jesus said unto them, Because of your unbelief: for verily I say unto you, if ye have faith a grain of a mustard seed, ye shall say unto this mountain, Remove hence to yonder place; and it shall remove; and nothing shall be impossible unto you. *Matt. 17:20*

Key Thought: Mustard seed faith is very powerful.

YOUR KEY
THOUGHT: _____
_____
_____
_____

YOUR PRAYER
REQUEST: _____
_____
_____
_____
_____
_____
_____
_____

DATES PRAYERS
ANSWERED: _____
_____
_____
_____

DAY 209

What things so ever ye desire, when ye pray, believer that ye receive them, and ye shall have them. *Mk.11:24*

Key Thought: Believe and receive whatever you pray for.

YOUR KEY
THOUGHT: _____
_____
_____
_____

YOUR PRAYER
REQUEST: _____
_____
_____
_____
_____
_____
_____
_____

DATES PRAYERS
ANSWERED: _____
_____
_____
_____

DAY 210

He that cometh to God must believe that he is, and that he is a rewarder of them that diligently seek him. *Heb. 11:6*

Key Thought: God is a rewarder to those that seek after him.

YOUR KEY
THOUGHT: _____
_____
_____
_____

YOUR PRAYER
REQUEST: _____
_____
_____
_____
_____
_____
_____
_____

DATES PRAYERS
ANSWERED: _____
_____
_____
_____

DAY 211

God is not a man that he should lie; neither the son of man, that he should repent; hath he said, and shall he not do it? or hath he spoken, and shall he make it good? *Num. 23:19*

Key Thought: God does not lie.

YOUR KEY
THOUGHT: _____
_____
_____
_____

YOUR PRAYER
REQUEST: _____
_____
_____
_____
_____
_____
_____
_____

DATES PRAYERS
ANSWERED: _____
_____
_____

DAY 212

Yea, I have spoken it, I will also bring it to pass; I have purposed it, I will also do it. *Is. 46:11*

Key Thought: God has a plan and a purpose.

YOUR KEY
THOUGHT: _____
_____
_____
_____

YOUR PRAYER
REQUEST: _____
_____
_____
_____
_____
_____
_____
_____

DATES PRAYERS
ANSWERED: _____
_____
_____
_____

DAY 213

Let us hold fast the profession of our faith without wavering, (for he is faithful that promised.) *Heb. 10:23*

Key Thought: Waver not in your faith.

YOUR KEY
THOUGHT: _____

_____

_____

_____

YOUR PRAYER
REQUEST: _____

_____

_____

_____

_____

_____

_____

_____

DATES PRAYERS
ANSWERED: _____

_____

_____

_____

DAY 214

For I the LORD thy God will hold thy right hand saying unto thee, Fear not; I will help thee. *Is. 41:13*

Key Thought: Hold to Gods unchanging hand.

YOUR KEY
THOUGHT: _____

_____

_____

_____

YOUR PRAYER
REQUEST: _____

_____

_____

_____

_____

_____

_____

_____

DATES PRAYERS
ANSWERED: _____

_____

_____

_____

DAY 215

And he said unto them, why are ye so fearful? how is it that ye have faith? *Mk.4:10*

Key Thought: Without faith, you become fearful.

YOUR KEY
THOUGHT: _____

_____

_____

_____

YOUR PRAYER
REQUEST: _____

_____

_____

_____

_____

_____

_____

_____

DATES PRAYERS
ANSWERED: _____

_____

_____

_____

DAY 216

Henceforth I call you not servants; for the servant knoweth not what his lord doeth: but I have called you friends; for all that I have heard of my Father I have made known unto you. *Jn.15:15*

Key Thought: We are friends of the Lord, whom he has kept no secrets.

YOUR KEY
THOUGHT: _____
_____
_____
_____

YOUR PRAYER
REQUEST: _____
_____
_____
_____
_____
_____
_____
_____

DATES PRAYERS
ANSWERED: _____
_____
_____
_____

DAY 217

A man that hath friends must shew himself friendly: and there is a friend that sticketh closer than a brother. *Prov.18:24*

Key Thought: The friendship between you and the Lord, is closer than you and you brother.

YOUR KEY
THOUGHT: _____
_____
_____
_____

YOUR PRAYER
REQUEST: _____
_____
_____
_____
_____
_____
_____
_____

DATES PRAYERS
ANSWERED: _____
_____
_____
_____

DAY 218

And he shall be like a tree planted by the rivers of water, that bringeth forth his fruit in his season; his leaf also shall not wither; and whatsoever he doeth shall prosper. *Ps. 1:3*

Key Thought: If you are rooted in Christ Jesus you will produce much fruit and shall prosper.

YOUR KEY
THOUGHT: _____
_____
_____
_____

YOUR PRAYER
REQUEST: _____
_____
_____
_____
_____
_____
_____
_____

DATES PRAYERS
ANSWERED: _____
_____
_____
_____

DAY 219

I, even, *am* he that blotted out thy transgressions for mine own sake, and will not remember thy sins. *Is. 43:25*

Key Thought: The Lord forgives and forgets.

YOUR KEY
THOUGHT: _____

_____
_____
_____

YOUR PRAYER
REQUEST: _____

_____
_____
_____
_____
_____
_____
_____

DATES PRAYERS
ANSWERED: _____

_____
_____
_____

DAY 220

For the LORD your God is gracious and merciful, and will not turn away his face from you, if ye return unto him. *2Chr.30:9*

YOUR KEY
THOUGHT: _____
_____
_____
_____

YOUR PRAYER
REQUEST: _____
_____
_____
_____
_____
_____
_____
_____

DATES PRAYERS
ANSWERED: _____
_____
_____
_____

DAY 221

As far as the east is from the west, so far hath he removed our transgressions from us.
Ps. 103:12

Key Thought: No matter how large the situation appears, He has forgiven us of our sins.

YOUR KEY
THOUGHT: _____
_____
_____
_____

YOUR PRAYER
REQUEST: _____
_____
_____
_____
_____
_____
_____
_____

DATES PRAYERS
ANSWERED: _____
_____
_____
_____

DAY 222

I will love thee, O LORD, my strength. The LORD *is* my rock, and my fortress, and my deliverer; my God, my strength, in whom I will trust; my buckler, and the horn of my salvation, and my high tower. I will call upon the LORD, who is *worthy* to be praised: so shall I be saved from mine enemies. *Ps. 18:1-3*

Key Thought: My Father, my strength, and my redeemer.

YOUR KEY
THOUGHT: _____
_____
_____
_____

YOUR PRAYER
REQUEST: _____
_____
_____
_____
_____
_____
_____
_____

DATES PRAYERS
ANSWERED: _____
_____
_____
_____

DAY 223

Rejoice not against me, O mine enemy: when I fall, I shall arise; when I sit in darkness, the LORD *shall* be a light unto me. *Mic. 7:8*

Key Thought: The Lord is my light when things seems dark.

YOUR KEY
THOUGHT: _____
_____
_____
_____

YOUR PRAYER
REQUEST: _____
_____
_____
_____
_____
_____
_____
_____

DATES PRAYERS
ANSWERED: _____
_____
_____
_____

DAY 224

The LORD is good, a strong hold in the day of trouble; and he knoweth them that trust in him. *Nah. 1:7*

Key Thought: The Lord my stronghold, in whom I trust.

YOUR KEY
THOUGHT: _____
_____
_____
_____

YOUR PRAYER
REQUEST: _____
_____
_____
_____
_____
_____
_____
_____

DATES PRAYERS
ANSWERED: _____
_____
_____
_____

DAY 225

Likewise the Spirit also helpeth our infirmities; for we know not what we should pray for as we ought: but the Spirit itself maketh intercession for us with groaning which cannot be uttered. *Rom.8:26*

Key Thought: The Holy Spirit will intercede on your behalf when the tongue fails.

YOUR KEY
THOUGHT: _____
_____
_____
_____

YOUR PRAYER
REQUEST: _____
_____
_____
_____
_____
_____
_____
_____

DATES PRAYERS
ANSWERED: _____
_____
_____
_____

DAY 226
And I will put my Spirit within you, and cause you to walk in my statutes and ye shall keep my judgement and do them. *Eze.36:27*

Key Thought: The Spirit of the Lord will cause you to walk upright and keep his commandments.

YOUR KEY
THOUGHT: _____
_____
_____
_____

YOUR PRAYER
REQUEST: _____
_____
_____
_____
_____
_____
_____
_____

DATES PRAYERS
ANSWERED: _____
_____
_____
_____

DAY 227

Believe in God, that raised him up from the dead, and gave him glory; that your faith and hope might be in God. *1Pet. 1:21*

Key Thought: Believe and have hope in God.

YOUR KEY
THOUGHT: _____
_____
_____
_____

YOUR PRAYER
REQUEST: _____
_____
_____
_____
_____
_____
_____
_____

DATES PRAYERS
ANSWERED: _____
_____
_____
_____

DAY 228

But let the righteous be glad; let them rejoice before God: yea, let them exceedingly rejoice. *Ps. 68:3*

Key Thought: Delight yourself before the Lord.

YOUR KEY
THOUGHT: _____
_____
_____
_____

YOUR PRAYER
REQUEST: _____
_____
_____
_____
_____
_____
_____
_____

DATES PRAYERS
ANSWERED: _____
_____
_____
_____

DAY 229

I will greatly rejoice in the LORD, my soul shall be joyful in my God; for he hath clothed me with the garments of salvation, he hath covered me with the robe of righteousness, as a bridegroom decketh himself with ornaments, and as a bride adorneth herself with her jewels. *Is. 61:10*

Key Thought: I have been clothed with the garment of salvation.

YOUR KEY
THOUGHT: _____
_____
_____
_____

YOUR PRAYER
REQUEST: _____
_____
_____
_____
_____
_____
_____
_____

DATES PRAYERS
ANSWERED: _____
_____
_____
_____

DAY 230

Then he said unto them, Go your way, eat the fat, and drink the sweet, and send portions unto them for whom nothing is prepared: for this day is holy unto our Lord: neither be ye sorry; for the joy of the LORD is your strength. *Neh. 8:10*

Key Thought: The joy of the Lord is your strength.

YOUR KEY
THOUGHT: _____
_____
_____
_____

YOUR PRAYER
REQUEST: _____
_____
_____
_____
_____
_____
_____
_____
_____

DATES PRAYERS
ANSWERED: _____
_____
_____
_____

DAY 231

Then shalt thou call, and the LORD shall answer, thou shalt cry, and he shall say, Here I am. *Is. 58:9*

Key Thought: Call on the Lord, and he shall answer.

YOUR KEY
THOUGHT: _____

_____

_____

_____

YOUR PRAYER
REQUEST: _____

_____

_____

_____

_____

_____

_____

_____

DATES PRAYERS
ANSWERED: _____

_____

_____

_____

DAY 232

But I am poor and needy; yet the LORD thinketh upon me. *Ps. 40:17*

Key Thought: The Lord loves all including the poor and the needy.

YOUR KEY
THOUGHT: _____
_____
_____
_____

YOUR PRAYER
REQUEST: _____
_____
_____
_____
_____
_____
_____
_____

DATES PRAYERS
ANSWERED: _____
_____
_____
_____

DAY 233

I will never leave you comfortless; I will come to you. *Jn. 14:18*

Key Thought: The Lord is always there.

YOUR KEY
THOUGHT: _____

_____
_____
_____

YOUR PRAYER
REQUEST: _____

_____
_____
_____
_____
_____
_____
_____

DATES PRAYERS
ANSWERED: _____

_____
_____
_____

DAY 234

I will heal their backsliding, I will love them freely; for mine anger is turned away from him.
Hosea 14:4

Key Thought: God gives healing love freely.

YOUR KEY
THOUGHT: _____
_____
_____
_____

YOUR PRAYER
REQUEST: _____
_____
_____
_____
_____
_____
_____
_____

DATES PRAYERS
ANSWERED: _____
_____
_____
_____

DAY 235

Beloved, let us love one another; for love is of God; and every one that loveth is born of God, and knoweth God. He that loveth not knoweth not God; for God is love. *1Jn 4:7-8*

Key Thought: God is love

YOUR KEY
THOUGHT: _____

_____

_____

_____

YOUR PRAYER
REQUEST: _____

_____

_____

_____

_____

_____

_____

_____

DATES PRAYERS
ANSWERED: _____

_____

_____

_____

DAY 236

The LORD openeth the eyes of the blind; the LORD raised them that are bowed down; the LORD loveth the righteous. *Ps 146:8*

Key Thought: I once was blind, but now I see. For the Lord opens the eyes of the blind.

YOUR KEY
THOUGHT: _____

_____

_____

_____

YOUR PRAYER
REQUEST: _____

_____

_____

_____

_____

_____

_____

_____

DATES PRAYERS
ANSWERED: _____

_____

_____

_____

DAY 237

But the meek shall inherit the earth; and shall delight themselves in the abundance of peace.
Ps. 37:11

Key Thought: Be meek and enjoy the abundance of peace.

YOUR KEY
THOUGHT: _____
_____
_____
_____

YOUR PRAYER
REQUEST: _____
_____
_____
_____
_____
_____
_____
_____

DATES PRAYERS
ANSWERED: _____
_____
_____
_____

DAY 238

And I thank Christ Jesus our Lord, who hath enabled me, for that he counted me faithful, putting me into the ministry. *1Tim.1:12*

Key Thought: Has Jesus counted you faithful?

YOUR KEY
THOUGHT: _____
_____
_____
_____

YOUR PRAYER
REQUEST: _____
_____
_____
_____
_____
_____
_____
_____

DATES PRAYERS
ANSWERED: _____
_____
_____
_____

DAY 239

And this gospel of the kingdom shall be preached in all the world for a witness unto all nations; and then shall the end come. *Matt. 24:14*

Key Thought: Preach the gospel of Jesus Christ to all the world.

YOUR KEY
THOUGHT: _____
_____
_____
_____

YOUR PRAYER
REQUEST: _____
_____
_____
_____
_____
_____
_____
_____
_____

DATES PRAYERS
ANSWERED: _____
_____
_____
_____

DAY 240

And the work of the righteousness shall be peace; and the effect of the righteousness quietness and assurance for ever. *Is. 32:17*

Key Thought: There is peace in the work of the righteous.

YOUR KEY
THOUGHT: _____
_____
_____
_____

YOUR PRAYER
REQUEST: _____
_____
_____
_____
_____
_____
_____
_____

DATES PRAYERS
ANSWERED: _____
_____
_____
_____

DAY 241

Now the Lord of peace himself give you peace always by all means. *2 Thess. 3:16*

Key Thought: The Lord is peace.

YOUR KEY
THOUGHT: _____

_____

_____

_____

YOUR PRAYER
REQUEST: _____

_____

_____

_____

_____

_____

_____

_____

DATES PRAYERS
ANSWERED: _____

_____

_____

_____

DAY 242

If my people, which are called by my name, shall humble themselves, and pray, and seek my face, and turn from their wicked ways, then will I hear from heaven, and will forgive their sin, and will heal their land. *2Chro.7:14*

Key Thought: Humble yourself, seek Christ, turn from your wicked ways, then you can be blessed.

YOUR KEY
THOUGHT: _____
_____
_____
_____

YOUR PRAYER
REQUEST: _____
_____
_____
_____
_____
_____
_____
_____

DATES PRAYERS
ANSWERED: _____
_____
_____
_____

DAY 243

For not the hearers of the law are just before God, but the doers of the law shall be justified.
Rom.2:13

Key Thought: Hearers and doers of the law alike shall be justified before God.

YOUR KEY
THOUGHT: _____
_____
_____
_____

YOUR PRAYER
REQUEST: _____
_____
_____
_____
_____
_____
_____
_____

DATES PRAYERS
ANSWERED: _____
_____
_____
_____

DAY 244
Keep therefore the words of this covenant, and do them that ye may prosper in all that ye do. *Deut. 29:9*

Key Thought: Obedience brings blessings and prosperity.

YOUR KEY
THOUGHT: _____
_____
_____
_____

YOUR PRAYER
REQUEST: _____
_____
_____
_____
_____
_____
_____
_____

DATES PRAYERS
ANSWERED: _____
_____
_____
_____

DAY 245

And the world passeth away, and the lust there of; but he that doeth the will of God abideth for ever. *1Jn. 2:17*

Key Thought: He that abides in the will of God shall remain forever.

YOUR KEY
THOUGHT: _____
_____
_____
_____

YOUR PRAYER
REQUEST: _____
_____
_____
_____
_____
_____
_____
_____

DATES PRAYERS
ANSWERED: _____
_____
_____
_____

DAY 246

And let us not be weary in well doing; for in due season we shall reap if we faint not.
Gal. 6:9

Key Thought: Do not give in to your situation, for you shall reap in your season.

YOUR KEY
THOUGHT: _____
_____
_____
_____

YOUR PRAYER
REQUEST: _____
_____
_____
_____
_____
_____
_____
_____

DATES PRAYERS
ANSWERED: _____
_____
_____
_____

DAY 247

The harvest truly is great, but the labourers are few, pray ye therefore the Lord of the harvest that he would send forth labourers into his harvest. *Lk. 10:2*

Key Thought: Are you willing to labour for the Lord?

YOUR KEY
THOUGHT: _____

_____

_____

_____

YOUR PRAYER
REQUEST: _____

_____

_____

_____

_____

_____

_____

_____

DATES PRAYERS
ANSWERED: _____

_____

_____

_____

DATE_____

DAY 248

For ye have need of patience, that after ye have done the will of God, ye might receive the promise. *Heb. 10:36*

Key Thought: Wait on the promise.

YOUR KEY
THOUGHT: _____
_____
_____
_____

YOUR PRAYER
REQUEST: _____
_____
_____
_____
_____
_____
_____
_____

DATES PRAYERS
ANSWERED: _____
_____
_____
_____

DAY 249

Sing unto the LORD, praise ye the LORD: for he hath delivered the sons of the poor from the hand of the evildoers. *Jerm. 20:13*

Key Thought: The poor shall be delivered from evildoers.

YOUR KEY
THOUGHT: _____
_____
_____
_____

YOUR PRAYER
REQUEST: _____
_____
_____
_____
_____
_____
_____
_____

DATES PRAYERS
ANSWERED: _____
_____
_____
_____

DAY 250

Bring my soul out of prison, that I may praise thy name; the righteous shall compass me about; for thou shalt deal bountifully with me. *Ps. 142:7*

Key Thought: The Lord will deliver your soul out of bondage.

YOUR KEY
THOUGHT: _____
_____
_____
_____

YOUR PRAYER
REQUEST: _____
_____
_____
_____
_____
_____
_____
_____

DATES PRAYERS
ANSWERED: _____
_____
_____
_____

DAY 251

Charge them that are rich in this world, that they be not highminded, nor trust in uncertain riches, but in the living God, who giveth us richly all things to enjoy; *1Tim.6:17*

Key Thought: Be not fooled by the things of the world.

YOUR KEY
THOUGHT: _____
_____
_____
_____

YOUR PRAYER
REQUEST: _____
_____
_____
_____
_____
_____
_____
_____

DATES PRAYERS
ANSWERED: _____
_____
_____
_____

DAY 252

Blessed is he that considereth the poor: the LORD will deliver him in time of trouble. *Ps. 41:1*

Key Thought: When you give to the poor God will reward you.

YOUR KEY
THOUGHT: _____

_____

_____

_____

YOUR PRAYER
REQUEST: _____

_____

_____

_____

_____

_____

_____

_____

DATES PRAYERS
ANSWERED: _____

_____

_____

_____

DAY 253

He healeth the broken in heart, and bindeth up their wounds. *Ps 147:3*

Key Thought: God mends broken hearts.

YOUR KEY
THOUGHT: _____
_____
_____
_____

YOUR PRAYER
REQUEST: _____
_____
_____
_____
_____
_____
_____
_____

DATES PRAYERS
ANSWERED: _____
_____
_____
_____

DAY 254

Blessed are ye, when men shall hate you, and when they shall separate you *from their company,* and shall reproach you, and cast out your name as evil, for the Son of man's sake. *Lk. 6:22*

Key Thought: Blessed are you to be hated for Christ sake.

YOUR KEY
THOUGHT: _____
_____
_____
_____

YOUR PRAYER
REQUEST: _____
_____
_____
_____
_____
_____
_____
_____

DATES PRAYERS
ANSWERED: _____
_____
_____
_____

DAY 255

The young lions do lack, and suffer hunger; but they that seek the LORD shall not want any good thing. *Ps 34:10*

Key Thought: God rewards those that seek him.

YOUR KEY
THOUGHT: _____
_____
_____
_____

YOUR PRAYER
REQUEST: _____
_____
_____
_____
_____
_____
_____
_____

DATES PRAYERS
ANSWERED: _____
_____
_____
_____

DAY 256

Say ye to the righteous, that it shall be well with him; for they shall not eat the fruit of their doing. *Is.3:10*

Key Thought: Give honestly from the heart, and whatever you give you will reap in return.

YOUR KEY
THOUGHT: _____
_____
_____
_____

YOUR PRAYER
REQUEST: _____
_____
_____
_____
_____
_____
_____
_____

DATES PRAYERS
ANSWERED: _____
_____
_____
_____

DAY 257

For the LORD knoweth the way of the righteous: but the way of the ungodly shall parish.
Ps. 1:6

Key Thought: The ungodly shall parish.

YOUR KEY
THOUGHT: _____
_____
_____
_____

YOUR PRAYER
REQUEST: _____
_____
_____
_____
_____
_____
_____
_____

DATES PRAYERS
ANSWERED: _____
_____
_____
_____

DAY 258

For this is good and acceptable in the sight of God our Savior; who will have all me to be saved and to come unto the knowledge of the truth. *1Tim. 2:34*

Key Thought: God's desire is that all men be saved and know His truth through His Son Jesus.

YOUR KEY
THOUGHT: _____
_____
_____
_____

YOUR PRAYER
REQUEST: _____
_____
_____
_____
_____
_____
_____
_____

DATES PRAYERS
ANSWERED: _____
_____
_____
_____

DAY 259

But if the wicked will turn from all his sins that he hath committed, and keep all my statues, and do that which is lawful and right, he shall surely live, he shall not die. *Ezek.18:21*

Key Thought: REPENT

YOUR KEY
THOUGHT: _____

_____

_____

_____

YOUR PRAYER
REQUEST: _____

_____

_____

_____

_____

_____

_____

_____

DATES PRAYERS
ANSWERED: _____

_____

_____

_____

DATE_____

DAY 260
For I am not come to call the righteous, but sinners to repentance. *Matt. 9:13*

Key Thought: Jesus came for the sinners.

YOUR KEY
THOUGHT: _____
_____
_____
_____

YOUR PRAYER
REQUEST: _____
_____
_____
_____
_____
_____
_____
_____

DATES PRAYERS
ANSWERED: _____
_____
_____
_____

DAY 261

Not by works of righteousness which we have done, but according to his mercy he saved us, by the washing of regeneration, and renewing of the Holy Ghost; *Titus 3:5*

Key Thought: Salvation is a gift to us.

YOUR KEY
THOUGHT: _____
_____
_____
_____

YOUR PRAYER
REQUEST: _____
_____
_____
_____
_____
_____
_____
_____

DATES PRAYERS
ANSWERED: _____
_____
_____
_____

DAY 262

Therefore if any man be in Christ, *he is* a new creature: old things are passed away; be hold, all things are become new. *2Cor. 5:17*

Key Thought: In Christ Jesus we are new, with a new life.

YOUR KEY
THOUGHT: _____
_____
_____
_____

YOUR PRAYER
REQUEST: _____
_____
_____
_____
_____
_____
_____
_____

DATES PRAYERS
ANSWERED: _____
_____
_____
_____

DAY 263

The LORD is with you, while ye be with him; and if ye seek him, he will be found of you; but if ye forsake him, he will forsake you. *2Chron. 15:2*

Key Thought: Seek the Lord, he will be there for you.

YOUR KEY
THOUGHT: _____

_____

_____

_____

YOUR PRAYER
REQUEST: _____

_____

_____

_____

_____

_____

_____

_____

DATES PRAYERS
ANSWERED: _____

_____

_____

_____

DAY 264

And the prayer of faith shall save the sick, and the Lord shall raise him up; and if he have committed sins, they shall be forgiven him. *James 5:15*

Key Thought: Pray in faith.

YOUR KEY
THOUGHT: _____
_____
_____
_____

YOUR PRAYER
REQUEST: _____
_____
_____
_____
_____
_____
_____
_____

DATES PRAYERS
ANSWERED: _____
_____
_____
_____

DAY 265

But *he was* wounded for our transgressions, *he was* bruised for our iniquities: the chastisement of our peace *was* upon him; and with stripes we are healed. *Is.53:5*

Key Thought: Jesus suffered for us.

YOUR KEY
THOUGHT: _____
_____
_____
_____

YOUR PRAYER
REQUEST: _____
_____
_____
_____
_____
_____
_____
_____

DATES PRAYERS
ANSWERED: _____
_____
_____
_____

DAY 266

Thou shalt not bow down to their gods, nor serve them, nor do after their works: but thou shalt utterly overthrow them, and quite break down their images.

And ye shall serve the LORD your God, and he shall bless thy bread, and thy water; and I will take sickness away from the midst of thee. *Ex.23:24-25*

Key Thought: Serve no others, but Our Lord thy God, and you shall be blessed.

YOUR KEY
THOUGHT: _____
_____
_____
_____

YOUR PRAYER
REQUEST: _____
_____
_____
_____
_____
_____
_____
_____

DATES PRAYERS
ANSWERED: _____
_____
_____
_____

DAY 267

Neither yield ye your members *as* instruments of unrighteousness unto sin: but yield your-selves unto God, as those that are alive from the dead, and your members *as* instruments of righteousness unto God.

For sin shall not have dominion over you: for ye are not under the law, but under grace. *Rom.. 6:13-14*

Key Thought: God's grace frees us from the enemies of sin.

YOUR KEY
THOUGHT: _____

_____

_____

_____

YOUR PRAYER
REQUEST: _____

_____

_____

_____

_____

_____

_____

_____

DATES PRAYERS
ANSWERED: _____

_____

_____

_____

DATE_____

DAY 268
THIS *IS* THE COVENANT THAT I WILL MAKE WITH THEM AFTER THOSE
DAYS, SAITH THE LORD, I WILL PUT MY LAWS INTO THEIR HEARTS, AND
IN THEIR MINDS WILL I WRITE THEM;
AND THEIR SINS AND INIQUITIES WILL I REMEMBER NO MORE.
Hew. 10:16-17

Key Thought: God's covenant separates us from sin.

YOUR KEY
THOUGHT: _____
_____
_____
_____

YOUR PRAYER
REQUEST: _____
_____
_____
_____
_____
_____
_____
_____

DATES PRAYERS
ANSWERED: _____
_____
_____
_____

DAY 269

If we confess our sins, he is faithful and just to forgive us our sins, and to cleanse us from all unrighteousness. *1John 1:9*

Key Thought: Repent, Jesus is faithful and just to forgive.

YOUR KEY
THOUGHT: _____
_____
_____
_____

YOUR PRAYER
REQUEST: _____
_____
_____
_____
_____
_____
_____
_____

DATES PRAYERS
ANSWERED: _____
_____
_____

DAY 270

And all these blessings shall come on thee, and over take thee, if thou shalt hearken diligently unto the voice of the LORD thy God, to *observe and* to do all his commandments which I command thee this day, that the LORD thy God will set thee on high above all nations of the earth:

And all these blessings shall come on thee, and overtake thee, if thou shalt hearken unto the voice of the LORD thy God

Blessed *shalt thou* be in the city, and blessed *shalt thou* be in the field.

Blessed *shall be* the fruit of thy body, and the fruit of thy ground, and the fruit of thy cattle, the increase of thy kine, and the flocks of thy sheep

Blessed *shall be* thy basket and thy store.

Blessed *shalt thou* be when thou comest in, and blessed shalt thou be when thou goest out. *Deut. 28:1-6*

Key Thought: Your blessings come when you listen to the voice of the Lord.

YOUR KEY
THOUGHT: _____
_____
_____
_____

YOUR PRAYER
REQUEST: _____
_____
_____
_____
_____
_____
_____
_____

DATES PRAYERS
ANSWERED: _____
_____
_____
_____

DAY 271

And our hope of you is stedfast, knowing, that as ye are partakers of the suffering, so shall ye be also of the consolation. *2Cor, 1:7*

Key Thought: Along with suffering there are consolations.

YOUR KEY
THOUGHT: _____

_____

_____

_____

YOUR PRAYER
REQUEST: _____

_____

_____

_____

_____

_____

_____

_____

DATES PRAYERS
ANSWERED: _____

_____

_____

_____

DAY 272

Beloved, think it is not strange concerning the fiery trial which is to try you, as though some strange thing happened unto you: but rejoice, inasmuch as ye are partakers of Christ suffering; that when his glory shall be revealed ye may one glad also with exceeding joy. *1Pet.4:12:13*

Key Thought: No matter what is before us, when Christ glory is revealed we should be exceedingly joyful.

YOUR KEY
THOUGHT: _____
_____
_____
_____

YOUR PRAYER
REQUEST: _____
_____
_____
_____
_____
_____
_____
_____

DATES PRAYERS
ANSWERED: _____
_____
_____
_____

DAY 273

Blessed be God even the Father of our Lord Jesus Christ, the Father of mercies, and the God of all comfort;

Who comforteth us in all our tribulation, that we may be able to comfort them which are in any trouble, by the comfort, wherewith we ourselves are comforted of God. *2 Corn. 1:3-4*

Key Thought: Comfort others as God so comfort us.

YOUR KEY
THOUGHT: _____

_____

_____

_____

YOUR PRAYER
REQUEST: _____

_____

_____

_____

_____

_____

_____

_____

DATES PRAYERS
ANSWERED: _____

_____

_____

_____

DAY 274

For unto you it is given in the behalf of Christ not only to believe on him, but also to suffer for his sake. *Philip. 1:29*

Key Thought: We must suffer for Christ sake.

YOUR KEY
THOUGHT: _____
_____
_____
_____

YOUR PRAYER
REQUEST: _____
_____
_____
_____
_____
_____
_____
_____

DATES PRAYERS
ANSWERED: _____
_____
_____
_____

DAY 275

Blessed is the man that endureth temptation: for when he is tried, he shall receive the crown of life, which the Lord hath promised to them that love him. *James 1:12*

Key Thought: Endure temptation and receive the crown of life.

YOUR KEY
THOUGHT: _____
_____
_____
_____

YOUR PRAYER
REQUEST: _____
_____
_____
_____
_____
_____
_____
_____
_____

DATES PRAYERS
ANSWERED: _____
_____
_____
_____

DAY 276

Fear not, little flock; for it is your Father's good pleasure to give you the kingdom. *Lk.12:32*

Key Thought: It is Gods pleasure that we receive the kingdom.

YOUR KEY
THOUGHT: _____
_____
_____
_____

YOUR PRAYER
REQUEST: _____
_____
_____
_____
_____
_____
_____
_____

DATES PRAYERS
ANSWERED: _____
_____
_____
_____

DAY 277

Therefore take no thought, saying, What shall we eat? or, What shall we drink? or Wherewithal shall we be clothed?

(For after all these things do the Gentiles seek:) for your heavenly Father knoweth that ye have need of all these things. *Matt. 6:31-32*

Key Thought: Do not fret about your needs, for Gods knows everything that you need.

YOUR KEY
THOUGHT: _____

_____

_____

_____

YOUR PRAYER
REQUEST: _____

_____

_____

_____

_____

_____

_____

_____

DATES PRAYERS
ANSWERED: _____

_____

_____

_____

DAY 278

I am come a light into the world, that whosoever believeth on me should not abide in darkness. *Jn. 12:46*

Key Thought: Abide in the light, do not live in darkness.

YOUR KEY
THOUGHT: _____
_____
_____
_____

YOUR PRAYER
REQUEST: _____
_____
_____
_____
_____
_____
_____
_____
_____

DATES PRAYERS
ANSWERED: _____
_____
_____
_____

DAY 279

So that we may boldly say, the Lord is my helper, and I will not fear what man shall do unto me. *Heb. 13:6*

Key Thought: Fear no man

YOUR KEY
THOUGHT: _____
_____
_____
_____

YOUR PRAYER
REQUEST: _____
_____
_____
_____
_____
_____
_____
_____

DATES PRAYERS
ANSWERED: _____
_____
_____
_____

DAY 280

For God giveth to a man that is good in his sight wisdom, and knowledge, and joy. *Eccles. 2:26*

Key Thought: God gives us wisdom, knowledge, and joy.

YOUR KEY
THOUGHT: _____
_____
_____
_____

YOUR PRAYER
REQUEST: _____
_____
_____
_____
_____
_____
_____
_____

DATES PRAYERS
ANSWERED: _____
_____
_____
_____

DAY 281

And he will teach us of his ways, and we will walk in his paths. *Is. 2:3*

Key Thought: Learn of Christ and be like him.

YOUR KEY
THOUGHT: _____

_____

_____

_____

YOUR PRAYER
REQUEST: _____

_____

_____

_____

_____

_____

_____

_____

DATES PRAYERS
ANSWERED: _____

_____

_____

_____

DAY 282

For the word of God is given, and powerful, and sharper than any two edged sword, piercing even to the dividing asunder of soul and spirit, and of the joints and marrows, and is a discerner of the thoughts and intents of the heart. *Heb. 4:12*

Key Thought: The word of God is power.

YOUR KEY
THOUGHT: _____
_____
_____
_____

YOUR PRAYER
REQUEST: _____
_____
_____
_____
_____
_____
_____
_____

DATES PRAYERS
ANSWERED: _____
_____
_____
_____

DAY 283

As new born babies desires the sincere milk of the word, that ye may grow there by:
1Pet. 2:2

Key Thought: Feeding off the word of God allow you to grow spiritually.

YOUR KEY
THOUGHT: _____

_____

_____

_____

YOUR PRAYER
REQUEST: _____

_____

_____

_____

_____

_____

_____

_____

DATES PRAYERS
ANSWERED: _____

_____

_____

_____

DAY 284

Ye are the light of the world. A city that is set on an hill cannot be hid. *Matt. 5:14*

Key Thought: You are a light shining in the midst of darkness.

YOUR KEY
THOUGHT: _____
_____
_____
_____

YOUR PRAYER
REQUEST: _____
_____
_____
_____
_____
_____
_____
_____

DATES PRAYERS
ANSWERED: _____
_____
_____
_____

DAY 285

For by thy words, thou shalt be justified, and by thy words thou shall be condemned. *Matt. 12:37*

Key Thought: The words we speak from our mouth, reflect the heart. For out of the abundance of the heart the mouth speaks.

YOUR KEY
THOUGHT: _____
_____
_____
_____

YOUR PRAYER
REQUEST: _____
_____
_____
_____
_____
_____
_____
_____

DATES PRAYERS
ANSWERED: _____
_____
_____
_____

DAY 286

But thou, when thou prayest, enter into thy closet, and when thou hast shut thy door, pray to thy Father which is in secret; and thy Father which seeth in secret shall reward thee openly. *Matt. 6:6*

Key Thought: Stop telling the devil your business. Stop confessing things that we fell are not right but go to God in prayer, and He will answer them.

YOUR KEY
THOUGHT: _____
_____
_____
_____

YOUR PRAYER
REQUEST: _____
_____
_____
_____
_____
_____
_____
_____

DATES PRAYERS
ANSWERED: _____
_____
_____
_____

DAY 287

And be not conformed to the world: but ye transformed by the renewing of your mind, that ye may prove what *is* that good, and acceptable, and perfect, will of God *Rom.12:2*

Key Thought: Do not live as the world live.

YOUR KEY
THOUGHT: _____
_____
_____
_____

YOUR PRAYER
REQUEST: _____
_____
_____
_____
_____
_____
_____
_____

DATES PRAYERS
ANSWERED: _____
_____
_____
_____

DAY 288

BRETHREN, If a man be overtaken in a fault, ye which are spiritual, restore such an one in the spirit of meekness; considering thyself, lest thou also be tempted. *Gal. 6:1*

Key Thought: If your brother falls comfort him with the word and restore his spirit.

YOUR KEY
THOUGHT: _____
_____
_____
_____

YOUR PRAYER
REQUEST: _____
_____
_____
_____
_____
_____
_____
_____

DATES PRAYERS
ANSWERED: _____
_____
_____
_____

DAY 289

And he shall bring forth thy righteousness as the light, and thy judgment as the noonday. *Ps. 37:6*

Key Thought: Your righteousness will be as the light.

YOUR KEY
THOUGHT: _____
_____
_____
_____

YOUR PRAYER
REQUEST: _____
_____
_____
_____
_____
_____
_____
_____

DATES PRAYERS
ANSWERED: _____
_____
_____
_____

DAY 290

Now also when I am old and greyheaded, O God, forsake me not; until I have shewed thy strength unto *this* generation, *and* thy power to everyone that is to come. *Ps 71:18*

Key Thought: Continue to do the will of God as you grow old, and God will continue to bless you.

YOUR KEY
THOUGHT: _____
_____
_____
_____

YOUR PRAYER
REQUEST: _____
_____
_____
_____
_____
_____
_____
_____

DATES PRAYERS
ANSWERED: _____
_____
_____
_____

DAY 291

And being found in fashion as a man he humble himself, and became obedient unto death, even the death of the cross. *Philp. 2:8*

Key Thought: Humble yourself, kill self, and live for Christ.

YOUR KEY
THOUGHT: _____

_____

_____

_____

YOUR PRAYER
REQUEST: _____

_____

_____

_____

_____

_____

_____

DATES PRAYERS
ANSWERED: _____

_____

_____

DATE_____

DAY 292

Your gold and silver is cankered; and the rust you, and shall eat your flesh as it were fire. Ye have heaped treasure together for the last day. *Jam.5:3*

Key Thought: Money and materialistic things shall be the cause of self- destruction.

YOUR KEY
THOUGHT: _____
_____
_____
_____

YOUR PRAYER
REQUEST: _____
_____
_____
_____
_____
_____
_____
_____

DATES PRAYERS
ANSWERED: _____
_____
_____
_____

DAY 293

For which cause we faint not; but though our outward man perish yet the inward man is renewed day by day. *2Corn. 4:16*

Key Thought: Your otter appearance will change daily with your spirit man daily.

YOUR KEY
THOUGHT: _____
_____
_____
_____

YOUR PRAYER
REQUEST: _____
_____
_____
_____
_____
_____
_____
_____

DATES PRAYERS
ANSWERED: _____
_____
_____
_____

DAY 294

The Spirit itself beareth witness, with our Spirit, that we are the children of God: *Rom. 8:16*

Key Thought: The Holy Spirit allows you to know that you are a child of God.

YOUR KEY
THOUGHT: _____
_____
_____
_____

YOUR PRAYER
REQUEST: _____
_____
_____
_____
_____
_____
_____
_____

DATES PRAYERS
ANSWERED: _____
_____
_____
_____

DAY 295

Let thy mercies come also unto me, O LORD, *even* thy salvation according to thy word. So shall I have wherewith to answer him that reproacheth me: for I trust in thy word. Ps. 119: 41-42

Key Thought: Trust in the word.

YOUR KEY
THOUGHT: _____
_____
_____
_____

YOUR PRAYER
REQUEST: _____
_____
_____
_____
_____
_____
_____
_____

DATES PRAYERS
ANSWERED: _____
_____
_____
_____

DAY 296
And the LORD shall make thee the head, and not the tail; and thou shalt be above only, and thou shalt not be beneath; if that thou hearken unto the commandments of the LORD thy God, which I command the this day to observe and to do them. *Deut.28:13*

Key Thought: Keep the Lord's commandments.

YOUR KEY
THOUGHT: _____
_____
_____
_____

YOUR PRAYER
REQUEST: _____
_____
_____
_____
_____
_____
_____
_____

DATES PRAYERS
ANSWERED: _____
_____
_____
_____

DAY 297

For God hath not given us the spirit of fear, but of power, and of love, and of a sound mind. *2Tim. 1:7*

Key Thought: Fear not though the Spirit, for though the spirit we have power, love, and a peaceful mind.

YOUR KEY
THOUGHT: _____
_____
_____
_____

YOUR PRAYER
REQUEST: _____
_____
_____
_____
_____
_____
_____
_____

DATES PRAYERS
ANSWERED: _____
_____
_____
_____

DAY 298

No weapon that is formed against me shall prosper; and every tongue *that* shall rise against thee in judgment thou shalt condemn. This *is* the heritage of the servant of the LORD, and their righteousness *is* of me, saith the LORD. *Is. 54:17*

Key Thought: Being a servant of God you have the inheritance of protection for anything that comes against you.

YOUR KEY
THOUGHT: _____
_____
_____
_____

YOUR PRAYER
REQUEST: _____
_____
_____
_____
_____
_____
_____
_____

DATES PRAYERS
ANSWERED: _____
_____
_____
_____

DAY 299

My little children, these things write I unto you, that ye sin not, And if any man sin, we have an advocate with the Father, Jesus Christ the righteous: *1Jn. 2:1*

Key Thought: Do not sin, but if you do go to Christ and repent.

YOUR KEY
THOUGHT: _____
_____
_____
_____

YOUR PRAYER
REQUEST: _____
_____
_____
_____
_____
_____
_____
_____

DATES PRAYERS
ANSWERED: _____
_____
_____

DAY 300

And these are they by the wayside, where the word is sown; but they have heard, Satan cometh immediately, and taketh away the word that was sown in their heart. *Mk. 4:15*

Key Thought: Be aware of Satan, for he comes to still what the Lord has spoken to you.

YOUR KEY
THOUGHT: _____
_____
_____
_____

YOUR PRAYER
REQUEST: _____
_____
_____
_____
_____
_____
_____
_____

DATES PRAYERS
ANSWERED: _____
_____
_____
_____

DAY 301

The thief cometh not, but for to steal, and to kill, and to destroy: I am come that they might have life, and that they might have it more abundantly. *Jn. 10:10*

Key Thought: The thief come to destroy the work of the Lord.

YOUR KEY
THOUGHT: _____
_____
_____
_____

YOUR PRAYER
REQUEST: _____
_____
_____
_____
_____
_____
_____
_____

DATES PRAYERS
ANSWERED: _____
_____
_____
_____

DAY 302

But they that wait upon the LORD shall renew *their* strength; they shall mount up with wings as eagles; they shall run, and not be weary; and they shall walk, and not faint. *Is. 40:31*

Key Thought: Wait on the Lord.

YOUR KEY
THOUGHT: _____
_____
_____
_____

YOUR PRAYER
REQUEST: _____
_____
_____
_____
_____
_____
_____
_____

DATES PRAYERS
ANSWERED: _____
_____
_____
_____

DAY 303
Rejoice in the Lord always: and again I say Rejoice. *Philp. 4:4*

Key Thought: Rejoice in the Lord.

YOUR KEY
THOUGHT: _____
_____
_____
_____

YOUR PRAYER
REQUEST: _____
_____
_____
_____
_____
_____
_____
_____

DATES PRAYERS
ANSWERED: _____
_____
_____
_____

DAY 304

And the peace of God, which passeth all understanding, shall keep your hearts and minds though Christ Jesus. *Philp. 4:7*

Key Thought: The peace of God will keep you.

YOUR KEY
THOUGHT: _____
_____
_____
_____

YOUR PRAYER
REQUEST: _____
_____
_____
_____
_____
_____
_____
_____

DATES PRAYERS
ANSWERED: _____
_____
_____
_____

DAY 305

Give, and it shall be given unto you; good measure, pressed down, and shaken together, and running over, shall men give into your bosom. For with the same measure that ye mete withal it shall be measured to you again. *Lk. 6:38*

Key Thought: When you give God will cause others to give to you.

YOUR KEY
THOUGHT: _____
_____
_____
_____

YOUR PRAYER
REQUEST: _____
_____
_____
_____
_____
_____
_____
_____

DATES PRAYERS
ANSWERED: _____
_____
_____
_____

DAY 306

And he said unto them, Go ye into all the world, and preach the gospel to every creature.
He that believeth and is baptized shall be saved; but he that believeth not shall be damned.
And these signs shall follow them that believe; In my name shall they cast out devils; they shall speak with new tongues;
They shall take up serpents; and if they drink any deadly thing, it shall not hurt them; they shall lay hands on the sick, and they shall recover. *Mk. 16:17-18*

Key Thought: The Great Commission.

YOUR KEY
THOUGHT: _____
_____
_____
_____

YOUR PRAYER
REQUEST: _____
_____
_____
_____
_____
_____
_____
_____

DATES PRAYERS
ANSWERED: _____
_____
_____
_____

DAY 307

Ye are of God, little children, and have overcome them: because greater is he that is in you, than he that is in the world. *1Jn. 4:4*

Key Thought: You can over come any obstacle that the devil put before you because of Christ Jesus that lives within you.

YOUR KEY
THOUGHT: _____
_____
_____
_____

YOUR PRAYER
REQUEST: _____
_____
_____
_____
_____
_____
_____
_____

DATES PRAYERS
ANSWERED: _____
_____
_____
_____

DAY 308

And David was greatly distressed; for the people spake of stoning him, because the soul of all the people was grieved, every man for his sons and for his daughters: but David encourage himself in the LORD his God. *1Sam. 30:6*

Key Thought: If no one else wants to praise the Lord, then you praise him all by yourself.

YOUR KEY
THOUGHT: _____
_____
_____
_____

YOUR PRAYER
REQUEST: _____
_____
_____
_____
_____
_____
_____
_____

DATES PRAYERS
ANSWERED: _____
_____
_____
_____

DAY 309

Can two walk together, except they be agreed? *Amos 3:3*

Key Thought: If there is no agreement, then there will be separation.

YOUR KEY
THOUGHT: _____
_____
_____
_____

YOUR PRAYER
REQUEST: _____
_____
_____
_____
_____
_____
_____
_____

DATES PRAYERS
ANSWERED: _____
_____
_____
_____

DAY 310

Take us the foxes, the little foxes, that spoils the vine: for our vines *have* tender grapes. *Song.2:15*

Key Thought: When young in the things of God, if we are not careful we can be easily turned back into the world.

YOUR KEY
THOUGHT: _____
_____
_____
_____

YOUR PRAYER
REQUEST: _____
_____
_____
_____
_____
_____
_____
_____

DATES PRAYERS
ANSWERED: _____
_____
_____
_____

DAY 311

The wolf also shall dwell with the lamb, and the leopard shall lie down with the kid; and the calf and the young lion and the fatling together; and a little child shall lead them. *Is. 11:6*

Key Thought: Listen to what your children are saying. God speaks to them also.

YOUR KEY
THOUGHT: _____
_____
_____
_____

YOUR PRAYER
REQUEST: _____
_____
_____
_____
_____
_____
_____
_____

DATES PRAYERS
ANSWERED: _____
_____
_____
_____

DAY 312

BE YE ANGRY, AND SIN NOT: let not the sun go down upon your wrath: *Eph. 4:26*

Key Thought: It's ok to get angry, but get it right before the day is over.

YOUR KEY
THOUGHT: _____
_____
_____
_____

YOUR PRAYER
REQUEST: _____
_____
_____
_____
_____
_____
_____
_____

DATES PRAYERS
ANSWERED: _____
_____
_____
_____

DAY 313

Confess *your* faults one to another, and pray one for another, that ye may be healed. The effectual fervent prayer of a righteous man availeth much. *Jam. 5:16*

Key Thought: When one stumbles pray for them with a sincere heart that they sin no more.

YOUR KEY
THOUGHT: _____
_____
_____
_____

YOUR PRAYER
REQUEST: _____
_____
_____
_____
_____
_____
_____
_____

DATES PRAYERS
ANSWERED: _____
_____
_____
_____

DAY 314

For God sent not his Son into the world to condemn the world; but that the world through him might be saved. *Jn. 3:17*

Key Thought: Jesus came that we might receive him.

YOUR KEY
THOUGHT: _____
_____
_____
_____

YOUR PRAYER
REQUEST: _____
_____
_____
_____
_____
_____
_____
_____

DATES PRAYERS
ANSWERED: _____
_____
_____
_____

DAY 315

Jesus said unto her, I am the resurrection, and the life: he that believeth in me, though he were dead, yet shall he live. *Jn. 11:25*

Key Thought: Jesus died and rose again that we might live.

YOUR KEY
THOUGHT: _____

_____

_____

_____

YOUR PRAYER
REQUEST: _____

_____

_____

_____

_____

_____

_____

_____

DATES PRAYERS
ANSWERED: _____

_____

_____

DAY 316

Jesus saith unto him, I am the way, the truth, and the life: no man cometh unto the Father, but by me. *Jn. 14:6*

Key Thought: Jesus is our mediator to the Father.

YOUR KEY
THOUGHT: _____
_____
_____
_____

YOUR PRAYER
REQUEST: _____
_____
_____
_____
_____
_____
_____
_____

DATES PRAYERS
ANSWERED: _____
_____
_____
_____

DAY 317

I WAS glad when they said unto me, Let us go into the house of the LORD. *Ps.122:1*

Key Thought: Be eager to get into the service of the Lord.

YOUR KEY
THOUGHT: _____
_____
_____
_____

YOUR PRAYER
REQUEST: _____
_____
_____
_____
_____
_____
_____
_____

DATES PRAYERS
ANSWERED: _____
_____
_____
_____

DAY 318

O magnify the LORD with me, and let us exalt his name together. *Ps. 34:3*

Key Thought: Tell someone about the goodness of God and together give him praise.

YOUR KEY
THOUGHT: _____

_____

_____

_____

YOUR PRAYER
REQUEST: _____

_____

_____

_____

_____

_____

_____

_____

DATES PRAYERS
ANSWERED: _____

_____

_____

_____

DAY 319

Is anything too hard for the LORD? At the time appointed I will return unto thee, according to the time of life, and Sarah shall have a son. *Gen. 18:14*

Key Thought: There is nothing to hard for God. Go to the Lord in prayer.

YOUR KEY
THOUGHT: _____
_____
_____
_____

YOUR PRAYER
REQUEST: _____
_____
_____
_____
_____
_____
_____
_____

DATES PRAYERS
ANSWERED: _____
_____
_____
_____

DAY 320

But ye are a chosen generation, a royal priesthood, an holy nation, a peculiar people; that ye should shew forth the praises of him who hath called you out of darkness into his marvelous. *1 Pet. 2:9*

Key Thought : Because of who we are in Christ Jesus we are a peculiar people.

YOUR KEY
THOUGHT: _____
_____
_____
_____

YOUR PRAYER
REQUEST: _____
_____
_____
_____
_____
_____
_____
_____

DATES PRAYERS
ANSWERED: _____
_____
_____
_____

DAY 321

And if it seem evil unto you to serve the LORD, choose you this day whom ye will serve; whether the gods which your fathers served that *were* on the other side of the flood, or the gods of the Am'-or-ites, in whose land ye dwell: but as for me and my house we will serve the LORD. *Josh. 24:15*

Key Thought: Everyone should chose to serve the Lord.

YOUR KEY
THOUGHT: _____

_____

_____

_____

YOUR PRAYER
REQUEST: _____

_____

_____

_____

_____

_____

_____

_____

DATES PRAYERS
ANSWERED: _____

_____

_____

_____

DAY 322

Neither give place to the devil. *Eph.4:27*

Key Thought: Do not allow yourself to be put into situations, which you can be tempted by the Satan.

YOUR KEY
THOUGHT: _____
_____
_____
_____

YOUR PRAYER
REQUEST: _____
_____
_____
_____
_____
_____
_____
_____

DATES PRAYERS
ANSWERED: _____
_____
_____
_____

DAY 323

For his anger *endureth but* a moment; in his favour *is* life: weeping may endure for a night, but joy *cometh* in the morning. *Ps. 30:5*

Key Thought: Because of Gods favor, joy comes in the morning.

YOUR KEY
THOUGHT: _____

_____

_____

_____

YOUR PRAYER
REQUEST: _____

_____

_____

_____

_____

_____

_____

_____

DATES PRAYERS
ANSWERED: _____

_____

_____

_____

DAY 324

For as he thinketh in his heart, so is he: Eat and drink. saith he to thee; but his heart is not thee. *Prov. 23:7*

Key Thought: Whatever is in your heart, that's what you are.

YOUR KEY
THOUGHT: _____
_____
_____
_____

YOUR PRAYER
REQUEST: _____
_____
_____
_____
_____
_____
_____
_____
_____

DATES PRAYERS
ANSWERED: _____
_____
_____
_____

DAY 325

Then said Jesus unto them, Yet a little while am I with you, and *then* I go unto him that sent me,

Ye shall seek *me*, and shall not find me: and where I am, *thither* ye cannot come.

Jn. 7:33-34

Key Thought: When Jesus returns it will be to late to seek him.

YOUR KEY
THOUGHT: _____
_____
_____
_____

YOUR PRAYER
REQUEST: _____
_____
_____
_____
_____
_____
_____
_____

DATES PRAYERS
ANSWERED: _____
_____
_____
_____

DATE_____

DAY 326

Thy word *is* a lamp unto my feet, and a light unto my path. *Ps. 119:105*

Key Thought: The word will lead and direct your path.

YOUR KEY
THOUGHT: _____
_____
_____
_____

YOUR PRAYER
REQUEST: _____
_____
_____
_____
_____
_____
_____
_____

DATES PRAYERS
ANSWERED: _____
_____
_____
_____

DAY 327

Give not which is holy unto the dogs, neither cast ye your pearls before swine, lest they trample them under their feet, and turn again and rend you. *Matt. 7:6*

Key Thought: The word of God is a jewel, be careful who you associate yourself with.

YOUR KEY
THOUGHT: _____
_____
_____
_____

YOUR PRAYER
REQUEST: _____
_____
_____
_____
_____
_____
_____
_____

DATES PRAYERS
ANSWERED: _____
_____
_____

DAY 328

Then said the Lord unto me, Thou hast seen: for I will hasten my word to perform it. *Jer.1:12*

Key Thought: Know that the Lord will quickly and eagerly perform just what he says in his word.

YOUR KEY
THOUGHT: _____
_____
_____
_____

YOUR PRAYER
REQUEST: _____
_____
_____
_____
_____
_____
_____
_____

DATES PRAYERS
ANSWERED: _____
_____
_____
_____

DAY 329

For we must needs die, and *are* as water spilt on the ground, which cannot be gathered up again; neither doth God respect *any* person: yet doth he devise means, that his banished be not expelled from him. *2Sam.14:14*

Key Thought: God loves everyone, for what he do for one he will do the same for another.

YOUR KEY
THOUGHT: _____
_____
_____
_____

YOUR PRAYER
REQUEST: _____
_____
_____
_____
_____
_____
_____
_____

DATES PRAYERS
ANSWERED: _____
_____
_____
_____

DAY 330

My Son, if sinners entice thee, consent not. *Prov.1:10*

Key Thought: Do not give into Satan trickery.

YOUR KEY
THOUGHT: _____
_____
_____
_____

YOUR PRAYER
REQUEST: _____
_____
_____
_____
_____
_____
_____
_____

DATES PRAYERS
ANSWERED: _____
_____
_____
_____

DAY 331

Happy *is* the man that findeth wisdom, and the man *that* getteth understanding. *Prov. 3:13*

Key Thought: Be happy in the word of God.

YOUR KEY
THOUGHT: _____

_____
_____
_____

YOUR PRAYER
REQUEST: _____

_____
_____
_____
_____
_____
_____
_____

DATES PRAYERS
ANSWERED: _____

_____
_____
_____

DAY 332

Be ye not unequally yoked together with unbelievers: for what fellowship hath righteousness with unrighteousness? And what communion hath light with darkness? *2Cor.6:14*

Key Thought: You can not fellowship with those that are not walking in the light.

YOUR KEY
THOUGHT: _____
_____
_____
_____

YOUR PRAYER
REQUEST: _____
_____
_____
_____
_____
_____
_____
_____

DATES PRAYERS
ANSWERED: _____
_____
_____
_____

DAY 333

And he arose, and rebuked the wind, and said unto the sea, Peace, be still. And the wind ceased, and there was a great calm. *Mk. 4:39*

Key Thought: Whenever a storm comes, say with authority Peace be still, and it shall obey.

YOUR KEY
THOUGHT: _____
_____
_____
_____

YOUR PRAYER
REQUEST: _____
_____
_____
_____
_____
_____
_____
_____

DATES PRAYERS
ANSWERED: _____
_____
_____

DAY 334

I will say of the LORD, He is my refuge and my fortress: my God; in him will I trust. *Ps. 91:2*

Key Thought: The Lord my protector.

YOUR KEY
THOUGHT: _____
_____
_____
_____

YOUR PRAYER
REQUEST: _____
_____
_____
_____
_____
_____
_____
_____

DATES PRAYERS
ANSWERED: _____
_____
_____
_____

DATE_____

DAY 335

And be ye not drunk with wine, wherein is excess; but be filled with the Spirit. *Eph. 5:18*

Key Thought: Be drunk in the Holy Spirit.

YOUR KEY
THOUGHT: _____

_____

_____

_____

YOUR PRAYER
REQUEST: _____

_____

_____

_____

_____

_____

_____

_____

DATES PRAYERS
ANSWERED: _____

_____

_____

_____

DAY 336

Do all things without murmurings and disputings: *Phil.2:14*

Key Thought: Everything you do, do it without complaining or arguing.

YOUR KEY
THOUGHT: _____

_____

_____

_____

YOUR PRAYER
REQUEST: _____

_____

_____

_____

_____

_____

_____

_____

DATES PRAYERS
ANSWERED: _____

_____

_____

_____

DAY 337

BOAST not thyself of to morrow; for thou knowest not what a day may bring forth.
Prov. 27:1

Key Thought: Do not brag about tomorrow, for tomorrow takes care of itself.

YOUR KEY
THOUGHT: _____
_____
_____
_____

YOUR PRAYER
REQUEST: _____
_____
_____
_____
_____
_____
_____
_____

DATES PRAYERS
ANSWERED: _____
_____
_____
_____

DAY 338

Train up a child in the way he should go: and when he is old, he will not depart from it. *Prov.22:6*

Key Thought: Teach the children how to live for Christ.

YOUR KEY
THOUGHT: _____
_____
_____
_____

YOUR PRAYER
REQUEST: _____
_____
_____
_____
_____
_____
_____
_____

DATES PRAYERS
ANSWERED: _____
_____
_____
_____

DAY 339

And we know that all things work together for good to them that love God, to them who are called according to *his* purpose. *Rom. 8:28*

Key Thought: <u>Everything</u> works for the good.

YOUR KEY
THOUGHT: _____

_____

_____

_____

YOUR PRAYER
REQUEST: _____

_____

_____

_____

_____

_____

_____

_____

DATES PRAYERS
ANSWERED: _____

_____

_____

DAY 340

Praying us with much intreaty that we would receive the gift, and *take upon us* the fellowship of ministering to the saints.

And *this they did*, not as we hoped, but first gave their own selves to the Lord, and unto us by the will of God. *2Cor. 8:4-5*

Key Thought: Pray and receive Gods gifts giving yourself unto the Lord, and live by his will.

YOUR KEY
THOUGHT: _____
_____
_____
_____

YOUR PRAYER
REQUEST: _____
_____
_____
_____
_____
_____
_____
_____

DATES PRAYERS
ANSWERED: _____
_____
_____
_____

DAY 341

And let us not be weary in well doing: for in due season we shall reap, if we faint not. *Gal.6:9*

Key Thought: Do not get discourage your season will come.

YOUR KEY
THOUGHT: _____
_____
_____
_____

YOUR PRAYER
REQUEST: _____
_____
_____
_____
_____
_____
_____
_____

DATES PRAYERS
ANSWERED: _____
_____
_____
_____

DAY 342

Wherein ye greatly rejoice, though now for a season, if need be, ye are in heaviness through manifold temptation. *1Pet. 1:6*

Key Thought: Be glad, even when trouble appears, for your troubles are for a short time.

YOUR KEY
THOUGHT: _____
_____
_____
_____

YOUR PRAYER
REQUEST: _____
_____
_____
_____
_____
_____
_____
_____

DATES PRAYERS
ANSWERED: _____
_____
_____
_____

DAY 343

Peace I leave with you, my peace I give unto you: not as the world giveth, give I unto you. Let not your heart be troubled, neither let it be afraid. *Jn.14:27*

Key Thought: There is no need to have a troubled heart, for you have the peace of Jesus with you.

YOUR KEY
THOUGHT: _____

_____

_____

_____

YOUR PRAYER
REQUEST: _____

_____

_____

_____

_____

_____

_____

_____

DATES PRAYERS
ANSWERED: _____

_____

_____

_____

DAY 344

NOW faith is the substance of things hoped for, the evidence of things not seen.
Heb. 11:1

Key Thought: Faith is believing with surety of what we are hoping for and certainty of what we do not see.

YOUR KEY
THOUGHT: _____
_____
_____
_____

YOUR PRAYER
REQUEST: _____
_____
_____
_____
_____
_____
_____
_____

DATES PRAYERS
ANSWERED: _____
_____
_____
_____

DAY 345

Ye have heard that it hath been said, AN EYE FOR AN EYE, AND A TOOTH FOR A TOOTH:

But I say unto you, That ye resist not evil: but whosoever shall smite thee on thy right cheek, turn to him the other also. *Matt. 5:38-39*

Key Thought: do not be revengeful.

YOUR KEY
THOUGHT: _____

_____

_____

_____

YOUR PRAYER
REQUEST: _____

_____

_____

_____

_____

_____

_____

_____

DATES PRAYERS
ANSWERED: _____

_____

_____

_____

DAY 346

Ye have heard that it hath been said, THOU SHALT LOVE THY NEIGHBOUR, hate thine enemy.

But I say unto you, Love your enemies, bless them that curse you, do good to them that hate you, and pray for them which despitefully use you, and persecute you;

That ye may be the children of your Father which is in heaven: for he maketh his sun to rise on the evil and on the good, and sendeth rain on the just and on the unjust. *Matt.5:43-45*

Key Thought: Pray for those that persecute you. God will bless you and them.

YOUR KEY
THOUGHT: _____
_____
_____
_____

YOUR PRAYER
REQUEST: _____
_____
_____
_____
_____
_____
_____
_____

DATES PRAYERS
ANSWERED: _____
_____
_____
_____

DAY 347

The LORD *is* my shepherd; I shall not want. *Ps. 23:1*

Key Thought: Allow the Lord to lead you and you will not want.

YOUR KEY
THOUGHT: _____

_____

_____

_____

YOUR PRAYER
REQUEST: _____

_____

_____

_____

_____

_____

_____

_____

DATES PRAYERS
ANSWERED: _____

_____

_____

_____

DAY 348

I have been young, and *now* am old; yet have I not seen the righteous forsaken, nor his seed begging bread. *Ps. 37:25*

Key Thought: The Lord does not forsake the righteous.

YOUR KEY
THOUGHT: _____

_____

_____

_____

YOUR PRAYER
REQUEST: _____

_____

_____

_____

_____

_____

_____

_____

DATES PRAYERS
ANSWERED: _____

_____

_____

_____

DAY 349

And when ye stand praying, forgive, if ye have ought against any: that your Father also which is in heaven may forgive you your trespasses.

But if ye do not forgive, neither will your Father which is in heaven forgive your trespasses. *Matt. 11:25-26*

Key Thought: Forgive others so that the Lord will forgive you.

YOUR KEY
THOUGHT: _____

_____

_____

_____

YOUR PRAYER
REQUEST: _____

_____

_____

_____

_____

_____

_____

_____

DATES PRAYERS
ANSWERED: _____

_____

_____

_____

DAY 350

Make no friendship with an angry man; and with a furious man thou shalt not go; Lest thou learn his ways, and get a snare to thy soul. *Prov. 22:24-25*

Key Thought: You become like the company that you keep.

YOUR KEY
THOUGHT: _____
_____
_____
_____

YOUR PRAYER
REQUEST: _____
_____
_____
_____
_____
_____
_____
_____

DATES PRAYERS
ANSWERED: _____
_____
_____
_____

DAY 351

I have shewed you all things, how that so labouring ye ought to support the weak, and to remember the words of the Lord Jesus, how he said, it is more blessed to give than to receive. *Acts 20:35*

Key Thought: It is more blessed to give than receive.

YOUR KEY
THOUGHT: _____
_____
_____
_____

YOUR PRAYER
REQUEST: _____
_____
_____
_____
_____
_____
_____
_____

DATES PRAYERS
ANSWERED: _____
_____
_____
_____

DAY 352

Every good gift and perfect gift is from above, and cometh down from the Father of lights, with whom is no variableness, neither shadow of turning. *James 1:17*

Key Thought: Know that everything good and perfect comes from heaven above.

YOUR KEY
THOUGHT: _____
_____
_____
_____

YOUR PRAYER
REQUEST: _____
_____
_____
_____
_____
_____
_____
_____

DATES PRAYERS
ANSWERED: _____
_____
_____
_____

DAY 353

But let none of you suffer as a murderer, or as a thief, or as an evildoer, or as a busybody in other men's matters. *1Pet. 4:15*

Key Thought: To speak wrong of some one is to kill another ones character.

YOUR KEY
THOUGHT: _____
_____
_____
_____

YOUR PRAYER
REQUEST: _____
_____
_____
_____
_____
_____
_____
_____

DATES PRAYERS
ANSWERED: _____
_____
_____

DAY 354

Yet if *any man suffer* as a Christian, let him not be ashamed; but let him glorify God on this behalf. *1Pet. 4:16*

Key Thought: Glorify God at all times.

YOUR KEY
THOUGHT: _____
_____
_____
_____

YOUR PRAYER
REQUEST: _____
_____
_____
_____
_____
_____
_____
_____

DATES PRAYERS
ANSWERED: _____
_____
_____
_____

DAY 355

Sorrow *is* better than laughter: for by the sadness of the countenance the heart is made better. *Eccl. 7:3*

Key Thought: To be sorrow is better than to laugh. Your face may be sadden, but it sharpens your understanding.

YOUR KEY
THOUGHT: _____
_____
_____
_____

YOUR PRAYER
REQUEST: _____
_____
_____
_____
_____
_____
_____
_____

DATES PRAYERS
ANSWERED: _____
_____
_____
_____

DAY 356
A merry heart doeth good like a medicine: but a broken spirit drieth the bones.
Prov. 17:22

Key Thought: Happiness is like medicine to your spirit.

YOUR KEY
THOUGHT: _____
_____
_____
_____

YOUR PRAYER
REQUEST: _____
_____
_____
_____
_____
_____
_____
_____

DATES PRAYERS
ANSWERED: _____
_____
_____
_____

DAY 357

I WILL lift up mine eyes unto the hills, from whence cometh my help.
My help *cometh* from the LORD, which made heaven and earth. *Ps. 121:1-2*

Key Thought: Call on the Lord, when in trouble, for your help comes from the Lord.

YOUR KEY
THOUGHT: _____
_____
_____
_____

YOUR PRAYER
REQUEST: _____
_____
_____
_____
_____
_____
_____
_____
_____

DATES PRAYERS
ANSWERED: _____
_____
_____
_____

DAY 358

He that walketh uprightly walketh surely: but he that perverteth his ways shall be known.
Prov. 10:9

Key Thought: To be honest will allow you to be safe and secure, but to be dishonest will surely be revealed.

YOUR KEY
THOUGHT: _____
_____
_____
_____

YOUR PRAYER
REQUEST: _____
_____
_____
_____
_____
_____
_____
_____

DATES PRAYERS
ANSWERED: _____
_____
_____
_____

DAY 359

Be strong and of good courage, fear not, nor be afraid of them: for the LORD thy God, he *it is* that doth go with thee; he will not fail thee, nor forsake thee. *Deut. 31:6*

Key Thought: Be not afraid nor be discourage for the Lord who goes with you will not fail you nor forsake you.

YOUR KEY
THOUGHT: _____

_____

_____

_____

YOUR PRAYER
REQUEST: _____

_____

_____

_____

_____

_____

_____

_____

DATES PRAYERS
ANSWERED: _____

_____

_____

_____

DAY 360

Hatred stirreth up strifes: but love covereth all sins. *Prov. 10:12*

Key Thought: Hate brings about trouble, where as love forgives all wrongdoings,

YOUR KEY
THOUGHT: _____
_____
_____
_____

YOUR PRAYER
REQUEST: _____
_____
_____
_____
_____
_____
_____
_____

DATES PRAYERS
ANSWERED: _____
_____
_____
_____

DAY 361

For we brought nothing into *this* world, and *it is* certain we can carry nothing out. *1Tim.6:7*

Key Thought: Do not become overwhelmed with material thing of the world, for you can not take it with you.

YOUR KEY
THOUGHT: _____
_____
_____
_____

YOUR PRAYER
REQUEST: _____
_____
_____
_____
_____
_____
_____
_____

DATES PRAYERS
ANSWERED: _____
_____
_____
_____

DAY 362

Yea, though I walk through the valley of the shadow of death, I will fear no evil: for thou *art* with me; thy rod and thy staff they comfort me. *Ps. 23:4*

Key Thought: When walking in the midst of unbelievers, the evil doers, be not afraid, for the word of God and the Holy Spirit will keep you.

YOUR KEY
THOUGHT: _____
_____
_____
_____

YOUR PRAYER
REQUEST: _____
_____
_____
_____
_____
_____
_____
_____

DATES PRAYERS
ANSWERED: _____
_____
_____
_____

DAY 363

NOW THE JUST SHALL LIVE BY FAITH: BUT IF *ANY MAN* DRAW BACK, MY SOUL SHALL HAVE NO PLEASURE IN HIM. *Heb. 10:38*

Key Thought: When you start to wavier in your faith, God is not pleased.

YOUR KEY
THOUGHT: _____
_____
_____
_____

YOUR PRAYER
REQUEST: _____
_____
_____
_____
_____
_____
_____
_____
_____

DATES PRAYERS
ANSWERED: _____
_____
_____
_____

DAY 364

Watch ye, stand fast in faith, quit you like men, be strong. *1Cor. 16:13*

Key Thought: Watch and wait on the Lord in faith.

YOUR KEY
THOUGHT: _____
_____
_____
_____

YOUR PRAYER
REQUEST: _____
_____
_____
_____
_____
_____
_____
_____

DATES PRAYERS
ANSWERED: _____
_____
_____
_____

DAY 365

Wherefore, my beloved brethren, let every man be swift to hear, slow to speak, slow to wrath. *James 1:19*

Key Thought: Think before speaking.

YOUR KEY
THOUGHT: _____

_____
_____
_____

YOUR PRAYER
REQUEST: _____

_____
_____
_____
_____
_____
_____
_____

DATES PRAYERS
ANSWERED: _____

_____
_____
_____

DAY 366

Let us hear the conclusion of the whole matter: Fear God, and keep his commandments: for this *is* the whole *duty* of man. *Eccl. 12:13*

Key Thought: The whole duty of man is to fear God and keep his commandments.

YOUR KEY
THOUGHT: _____
_____
_____
_____

YOUR PRAYER
REQUEST: _____
_____
_____
_____
_____
_____
_____
_____

DATES PRAYERS
ANSWERED: _____
_____
_____
_____

The One on One with the Master is a personal Bible study.
2Tim.2:15 says to "Study to shew thyself approved unto God, a
workman that needeth not to be ashamed, rightly dividing the
word of truth." Therefore God has given us the Bible.
You will get to know God on a personal level you will
get to know him and doing His will.
This is why I believe devotional bible study is most important. In devotional
bible study we are reading and studying His word in order that we may hear His
voice, that we may know how to do His will and live a better Christian life.

Printed in the United States
By Bookmasters